YOU SHOULD TRY

A GUIDE FOR CANADIANS

Library and Archives Canada Cataloguing in Publication
Title: Wines you should try : a guide for Canadians.
Names: Phillips, Roderick, author.
Description: Written by Roderick Phillips.
Identifiers: Canadiana 20189069260 | ISBN 9781770503274 (softcover)
Subjects: LCSH: Wine and wine making—Canada. |
LCSH: Food and wine pairing—Canada. | LCSH: Wine and wine making. |
LCSH: Food and wine pairing.
Classification: LCC TP559.C3 P56 2019 | DDC 641.2/2—dc23

We acknowledge the financial support of the Government of Canada
Nous reconnaissons l'appui financier du gouvernement du Canada.

Canadä

We acknowledge the financial support of the Government of Canada through the Canada Book Fund (CBF) for our publishing activities and the Province of British Columbia through the Book Publishing Tax Credit.

Design: Tanya Montini
Printed in Canada.

www.whitecap.ca

Wines
YOU SHOULD TRY

A GUIDE FOR CANADIANS

ROD PHILLIPS

TABLE OF CONTENTS

Wine
is sunlight
held together
by water.

- GALILEO GALILEI

INTRODUCTION

This is the first wine guide written specifically for Canadians, no matter where in Canada they live. Unlike wine guides that focus on the wines available in one of Canada's provinces, this is a guide to quality and good-to-great-value wines that are widely available across the country. It includes wines of three colours—red, rosé, and white—and all styles, including still and sparkling wines, wines that are dry, off-dry, and sweet, and fortified wines such as sherry and port. If you drink wine, you'll find many wines here that suit your palate and are perfect for the occasion you're buying wine for.

I've been tasting thousands of wines each year for decades. There are great wines, excellent wines, very good and good wines, and also wines that are mediocre and poor—not to mention some that should never be on any market at any price. While preparing this guide, I tasted many more wines than I included and I selected those that I believe offer quality and value for the price.

Speaking of price: the cost of a bottle of wine is not necessarily a good guide to its quality. There are some really excellent wines under $12 and some not-so-good wines that cost a lot more than that. I haven't discriminated by price, and you'll find many wines here that are really inexpensive and good quality, as well as many in the higher price brackets.

Nor have I discriminated by producer. There's a

tendency in the wine world to look down on wines made for the mass market—wines made in the hundreds of thousands or millions of bottles—as if they couldn't possibly be as good as wine produced by winemakers making a few thousand cases of wine a year. But many of the big producers—whether they're in France, Italy, California, Argentina, Chile, or elsewhere—make excellent wines year after year. In this guide you find wines from these producers alongside wines made by mid-sized and small producers.

I'm happy to have feedback on the wines in this guide and suggestions of wines I should think of for the next edition. You can e-mail me at rodphillips@worldsofwine.com

Cheers!

Rod Phillips

HOW WERE THE WINES IN THIS GUIDE SELECTED?

For ten years I wrote the annual *500 Best-Value Wines in the LCBO*, which was a guide to the best-value wines in Ontario's provincial liquor system. Each spring I asked wine agencies and wineries to send me samples of the wines they wanted considered for inclusion in the guide. I did the same for the present guide, the one you have in your hands, and I received more than a thousand wines to consider.

I tasted all the wines systematically, all at the proper temperature: the reds cool, the whites and sparkling wines chilled. As I tasted, I made notes and triaged the wines: wines that would definitely make the cut, wines that might be in the guide, and wines that would definitely not make it. Unlike my guide to wines in the LCBO, which included 500 wines each year, I aimed for no particular number for this guide. If there were 200, fine. If there were 800, fine. As it turned out, there are 500.

I made no distinction in terms of style, and this guide is certainly not simply a list of the wines I like to drink. It's true that I like most of them, but there are some styles I'm not so keen on, such as very sweet wines and the sweeter red wines that have become quite popular. But a wine guide is not about personal preference, and I applied the same criteria to all the wines that I tasted: balance and quality.

Most wine professionals agree that balance is essential in wine, meaning that there should be a balance among all the components: fruit, acid, and alcohol, and (where appropriate) sugar and tannins. That means that when I taste sweet wines, such as icewines, I look not only for sweetness, but for the appropriate level of acidity and fruit flavour. Sweetness alone is not enough. When I taste dry wines, I look not only for good acidity, but evident fruit flavours. When I tasted big, robust, red wines, I look not only at their concentrated fruit flavours but also for the right level of acidity and structure that is needed to make them drinkable and go well with food.

The wines in this guide are balanced for the styles of wine they represent. Very sweet wines in this guide have good fruit and acidity. High-acid wines (such as some rieslings) have enough fruit to balance the acidity. The wines here do not smell or taste of alcohol, even if they have a high alcohol level. Fruit-driven wines have enough acidity to keep them fresh.

ARE THESE WINES AVAILABLE EVERYWHERE?

Relatively few wines are available in every province of Canada such wines are all imported, high-volume wines because it takes large volumes to supply wine-drinkers across Canada. That's why you'll find brands such as Wolf Blass (from Australia), Mouton Cadet (France), Woodbridge (California), Cono Sur (Chile), and Santa Julia (Argentina) almost everywhere in Canada. There's absolutely no problem with wines made in large volumes. Many wines from producers like these are very good quality, and many are listed in this guide for that reason.

But I wanted to dig deeper into the wines for sale in Canada. So instead of requiring wines to be available across Canada in order to be included in this guide, I made it a criterion that a wine must be available in at least two provinces. That extended the range of wines considerably. Here you'll find wines from Canada and all around the world, some of them available in only two provinces but the great majority of them available even more widely.

This means that no matter where you live in Canada, you'll find that many of the wines in this guide are available locally, either in a provincial liquor retail system, a private wine store, or in a supermarket.

The 'two-province rule' allowed many more wines into this guide, especially Canadian wines. Many British Columbia wineries sell their wines in Alberta and other western provinces, and others sell widely in central and eastern Canada, too. Likewise, many Ontario wines are available in markets such as Quebec, Manitoba, Alberta, British Columbia, and Nova Scotia. A few Nova Scotia wines are sold in other Atlantic provinces, and some are in markets elsewhere in Canada.

HOW TO READ THIS GUIDE

BRAND   STYLE/VARIETY   VINTAGE YEAR

Wolf Blass 'Yellow Label' Sauvignon Blanc 2016
Adelaide Hills, Mount Gambier 13% alc.   **$$**
This is a well-made sauvignon blanc with all the character and properties you look for in the variety.

APPELLATION/ORIGIN   ALCOHOL BY VOLUME   PRICE

HERE ARE SOME MORE DETAILED EXPLANATIONS
Vintage
The vintage of any wine denotes the year the vines produced the grapes used in the wine. The vintages given in this guide are the vintages of the wines that I tasted. Over time, of course, the vintages on the shelf change, as one vintage sells through and the next takes its place. This means that the vintage on the bottle you find might not be the same as the one in this guide.

Does that matter? It might, to the extent that many wines do vary from vintage to vintage, depending on the weather each year. A wine from a cooler year might have higher acidity and less concentrated fruit. A wine from a warmer year might have more fruit flavour and higher alcohol. Some regions vary more from year to year than others in terms of their weather. There is more vintage variation in wines from Ontario, for example, than wines from Argentina. At the same time some producers, especially of high-volume wines, try to minimize vintage variation and standardize style so that consumers are not surprised when they taste a new vintage.

My experience is that although many wines vary by vintage, producers of quality wine make quality wine year in and year out. The flavours and textures might be a bit different, but the basic style and the quality stay the same. To this extent the wine you buy might be somewhat different from the one I tasted, but I'm confident that the producers whose wines are in this guide make very good wines year after year.

Prices

Wine prices vary from province to province across Canada. They represent the basic cost of the wine, which is negotiated between the producer and the purchaser (such as a wine store or a provincial alcohol retailing system), together with taxes (which vary provincially), mark-ups, and margins. Rather than give the precise price of each wine in each province, I have used price bands, as follows:

$ = Under $12

$$ = $12-$20

$$$ = $20-$30

$$$$ = $30-$40

$$$$$ = over $40

In many cases I indicate two price bands (such as $$-$$$) because a wine falls with one price band in some provinces and in another price-band in others. Most of the wines in this book fall into the $$ and $$$ bands, between $12 and $30.

Provenance

The geographical provenance of each wine is shown in this guide as it appears on the label. Some refer to countries, provinces, and states, such as Chile, New Zealand, California, British Columbia, and South Australia. Others refer to smaller designated viticultural areas (appellations) such as Niagara Peninsula in Ontario, Coonawarra in South Australia, and Bordeaux in France. Some are even smaller, such as Médoc in Bordeaux and Niagara-on-the-Lake in Niagara Peninsula.

Some of these names are preceded by an abbreviation that represents the official classification of the wines, meaning that they have met the criteria needed to qualify for that designation. The criteria vary from place to place, but they generally require that the wine must be made from grapes grown in a specified region and that a minimum percentage of the wine must be the grape variety shown on the label. For example, a chardonnay labelled VQA Niagara Peninsula must be made from grapes grown there, and at least 85% of the wine must be chardonnay—up to 15% can be other varieties. Some regions require only 75% of the wine to be the variety on the label, so that a California cabernet sauvignon might have up to 25% other varieties, such as merlot. Some certifying bodies require wines to pass a tasting panel, others do not.

The most common abbreviations in this guide are:

AOC/AOP Appellation d'Origine Contrôlée/Protégée (France). The most rigorous level of approval given to wines in France, certifying that the wine has satisfied various requirements for the appellation it is labelled with (such as AOC Bordeaux)

BC VQA	British Columbia Vintners Quality Alliance. Wines labelled BC VQA must satisfy certain criteria and be approved by a tasting panel.
DO	Denominación de Origin, a term used in Spain and Chile, equivalent to AOC
DOC	Term used in Portugal and Italy, equivalent to AOC. Used in Spain to indicate a classification higher than DO.
DOCG	DOC e Garantita. Term used in Italy to indicate a classification higher than DOC.
IGT/IGP	Indication Géographique Typique/Protégée (France) and Indicazione Geografica Tipica/ Protetta (Italy). This signifies a regional wine that satisfies the requirements of the region it is labelled for.
VQA	Vintners Quality Alliance (Ontario). Wines labelled VQA must satisfy certain criteria and be approved by a tasting panel.
WO	Wine of Origin (South Africa) indicating a wine conforming to the rules of the wine region named.

Note that most New World countries show the place of origin on their wine labels but do not show the classification. Designated wine regions in the United States are called American Viticultural Areas (AVAs), but American wine labels rarely show the letters AVA with the name of origin. Labels read 'Napa Valley', not 'Napa Valley AVA'. The same is true of Australia and New Zealand, where wine regions are officially called Geographical Indications but wines are not labelled with the letters 'GI'.

Descriptions

In my description of each wine I have focused on style: whether the wine is light or full bodied; whether it is dry, off-dry, or sweet; whether it is lightly or highly acidic; how strong the tannins are.

I do not list flavours in the way that is very popular— describing wines as having citrus, dark plum, cherry, or apple flavours, as being peppery or spicy, or having notes of white flowers, smoke, and forest floor. These fruit, floral, spice, and other descriptors are very common but they are not very helpful if you are choosing wine. First, there is little agreement among wine writers when it comes to flavours. One writer might describe a wine as having floral notes and citrus and apple flavours, while another might describe it as tasting of peaches, lemon zest, and pears.

More important, no one buys wines by flavour. When you're thinking of choosing a wine to sip on the patio or to drink with dinner, you don't think, "I'd like a wine with lemon zest and green apple flavours to sip on the deck and one with dark cherry, plum, and peppery notes to drink with my steak." You think of a light, refreshing white wine for the patio and a full-bodied, dry red with firm tannins for dinner. In other words, you think of style, not flavours. The descriptions in this guide point you to the style you're looking for.

Why no scores?

Whether they are points out of a hundred or stars out of five, scores are only a quick guide to a wine reviewer's assessment of a wine. The description is far more useful because words are much more nuanced. When you see a wine described as 'elegant', 'lovely', or 'attractive', you get a clear idea what I think about the wines, and the description tells you why.

Wine and food

With the description of each wine I've suggested two or three foods I think would pair well. These are simply suggestions, and they're by no means exhaustive. There's a lot of nonsense written today about pairing food and wine—for centuries, until the 1970s, no one cared very much about pairing—and it's become highly overcomplicated.

There are a couple of simple guidelines. First, the food shouldn't overwhelm the wine and the wine shouldn't overwhelm the food. You won't taste a mild-flavoured wine if you drink it with highly seasoned food, and you won't taste delicately flavoured food if you eat it with a powerful, intensely flavoured wine. Second, spicy foods often go well with slightly sweet wines. Third, if you're pairing wine with dessert, the wine shouldn't be sweeter than the dessert.

Other than that, the old guideline of drinking red wines with red meat and white wines with white meat and fish works well most of the time.

The discovery of
a wine is of greater
moment than the
discovery of a
constellation.
The universe is
too full of stars.

– BENJAMIN FRANKLIN

WHITE WINES

Argento 'Selección' Chardonnay 2017

Argentina 13.5% alc. $$

This is a straightforward chardonnay that's simply well made, uncomplicated, and good value. The fruit flavours are bright and have decent complexity and they're well balanced by refreshing acidity that sets the wine up for food. At the table it's very versatile and goes with any fish, seafood, or poultry dish that's not too heavily seasoned.

Crios Torrontés 2017

Argentina 13.5% alc. $$

Torrontés (pronounced Toron-tess) is an aromatic grape variety of uncertain parentage that is quite widely grown in Argentina. This is a fine example made by Susana Balbo, one of the country's foremost winemakers. Look for spicy, slightly perfumed notes on the nose and lovely light spiciness in the flavours. The acidity is crisp and perfectly balanced. This is a wine you can enjoy on its own or with slightly spicy poultry, vegetarian and seafood dishes.

Hardys 'Stamp Series' Chardonnay-Semillon 2016
South Eastern Australia 13% alc. $$

South Eastern Australia is a massive wine zone that includes most of the country's vineyards. This blend, which is mostly chardonnay, expresses some complexity from the two varieties, including some brightness and textural character from the semillon. The flavours are vibrant, the acidity is refreshing, and the balance is very good. Sip it on its own or drink it with chicken or white fish dishes.

Lindeman's 'Bin 95' Sauvignon Blanc 2017
South Eastern Australia 12% alc. $$

This is an easy-drinking, fruity sauvignon blanc you can sip on its own or pair with a wide range of foods: fish and seafood, chicken, light-intensity curries, and mild cheeses. The flavours are bright and breezy and the acidity is clean and crisp. It's by no means a complicated sauvignon blanc, but it expresses the variety effectively.

McGuigan Pinot Grigio 2017
Australia 12% alc. $

This is a light-bodied, fruity pinot grigio that's an easy-drinking, year-round wine. It shows pleasant fruit flavours with just a hint of sweetness, and the right level of crisp acidity. It's far from being a complicated wine, but it's a good choice for a lower-alcohol, easy-going white wine. You can drink it on its own or with lighter foods such as roast chicken, fish and chips, and sushi.

Penfolds 'Koonunga Hill' Chardonnay 2016
South Australia 12.5% alc. $$

This is a fine chardonnay that shows balance and style across the board. The flavours are bright yet solid,

AUSTRALIA

Wolf Blass is an iconic Australian wine producer that makes wines not only for the mass market but also high-end, limited editions. Wolf Blass, who emigrated to Australia from Germany, founded the winery and made his wines distinctive by giving the labels specific colours, such as yellow, red, and green. He was inspired, he says, by the colours worn by jockeys on race horses so that they could be identified at a distance. Wolf Blass 'Yellow Label' wines are still easily recognizable on wine-store shelves, and although some of the other colours have been retired, platinum and black denote the upper tiers of Wolf Blass wines. The Wolf Blass winemaking team, led by Chris Hatcher and based in the Barossa Valley wine region, continues to produce high-quality wines.

persistent and layered, and they're complemented by well-tailored acidity. It's a serious but easy-drinking wine that you might drink on its own but that calls for food. Drink it with poultry and pork or with richer fish and seafood dishes—richer because they're liberally seasoned.

Rymill 'The Yearling' Sauvignon Blanc 2017
Coonawarra 11.8% alc. $$

The Coonawarra wine region, in South Australia, is best known for cabernet sauvignon, but it's clearly more than a one-trick pony—a reference you'll get when you see the label of this wine. It's a really lovely sauvignon blanc with fresh and complex flavours that are backed by bright, crisp acidity. This is a clear choice for seafood and white fish, and it also goes well with many poultry dishes and mild-to-medium curries.

Vassse Felix 'Filius' Chardonnay 2017
Margaret River 12.5% alc. $$$-$$$$

This is a really fine chardonnay that's a perfect companion for dishes like roasted chicken and turkey, grilled white fish, and medium-strength cheeses. There's a very attractive hint of oak in the aromas and flavours—just a soupçon and nothing to be afraid of, as it complements the elegant fruit very well. The acidity is well calibrated and the wine is harmonious and delicious. 'Felix' means 'happy' in Latin and this wine definitely makes me happy.

Wolf Blass 'Yellow Label' Chardonnay 2017
Padthaway, Adelaide Hills 13% alc. $$

This is an almost iconic chardonnay that has sold well as long as it's been on the market—and that's quite some time. It has evolved over time and has reached a point where it is sourced from two of Australia's top wine regions and delivers well-defined flavours with clean, brisk acidity. Overall it's well balanced and can be sipped on its own or drunk with a variety of foods: mild cheeses, chicken, and pork.

Wolf Blass 'Yellow Label' Sauvignon Blanc 2016
Adelaide Hills, Mount Gambier 13% alc. $$

This is a well-made sauvignon blanc with all the character and properties you look for in the variety. The flavours are bright, fresh, and consistent from start to finish, while the acidity is clean and refreshing and supports the fruit very well. It's a well-balanced wine and it goes well with the usual sauvignon blanc pairings: shellfish, seafood, white fish, goat cheese, and the like.

CANADA—BRITISH COLUMBIA

Clos du Soleil 'Capella' White 2016
BC VQA British Columbia 13.4% alc. $$$

This is a very attractive blend of sauvignon blanc (80%) and semillon (20%) that goes well with smoked white fish, creamy seafood pasta, and poultry. The flavours are slightly spicy and are consistent and focused from start to finish, while the acid is bright and clean. The semillon contributes a little weight to the texture, and it finishes light and fresh.

Diabolica White 2015
BC VQA Okanagan Valley 13% alc. $

This is a soft-textured, easy-drinking white blend that will please many palates. It's fruit-driven with flavours that are concentrated and persistent and have a hint of sweetness. The texture is plush, round, and mouth-filling and the acidity is soft but effective. You can certainly sit back and sip this white on its own, or you could drink it with many poultry dishes.

Five Vineyards Chardonnay 2015
BC VQA Okanagan Valley 13.7% alc. $$

Named for Mission Hill's five vineyard properties in the Okanagan Valley, this chardonnay can be sourced from one or more of them. What you get is a nicely made, very approachable chardonnay that's very versatile with food. It delivers bright, clean fruit backed by refreshing acidity and it's a very good partner for the usual suspects: poultry, white fish, and mild cheeses.

Five Vineyards Pinot Blanc 2016
BC VQA Okanagan Valley 13% alc. $$

Not a lot of Canadian wineries make wine from pinot blanc, so it's nice to see this one. The flavours are not too forward but well-defined and nicely layered, while the crisp acidity clicks in to make this a food-friendly and very drinkable white. Overall, it's a very attractive, medium-bodied white that goes well with white fish, chicken, many salads, and with mild-strength cheeses.

Five Vineyards Sauvignon Blanc 2016
BC VQA Okanagan Valley 13.5% alc. $$

The name refers to the five vineyards that Mission Hill, producer of this wine, cultivates in the Okanagan Valley. This is a lovely sauvignon blanc that presents fresh fruit flavours underpinned by quite vibrant acidity. It's a juicy-textured wine that goes well with many things from the seas, lakes, and rivers, as well as with salads. Try it with mussels in a garlic white wine sauce, frites, and a salad.

Mission Hill Reserve Chardonnay 2015
BC VQA Okanagan Valley 13.8% alc. $$$

This is a quite elegant chardonnay that shows quality across the board. The fruit is ripe, layered, and defined, and the spine of acidity is clean and vibrant. The texture is noteworthy for a degree of creaminess that provides a nice counterpoint to the edginess of the acidity. This goes well with richer foods that include scallops and lobster, as well as blanquette de veau and many poultry dishes.

Monte Creek Riesling 2016
BC VQA British Columbia 11% alc. $$

This is a lovely dry riesling with just the merest hint of sweetness. It's often the best style, because it gives the wine the versatility of the dry and off-dry styles without the sweetness of off-dry. The flavours are well defined and focused, and the acidity is fresh and lively. You can pair this with seafood, smoked salmon, and chicken or with slightly spicy dishes in one of the South-east Asian cuisines.

Quails' Gate Chardonnay 2016
BC VQA Okanagan Valley 13% alc. $$$

This is a really lovely—and above all drinkable—chardonnay that delivers across the board. It's medium bodied and shows concentrated, fresh, and well-layered fruit, along with refreshing acid. There's a hint of oak from old-barrel aging. The texture is what the French sometimes call salivant, meaning that it makes you salivate—a good thing, as it sets you up for food. As for food, enjoy this chardonnay with roast poultry and grilled white fish.

Quails' Gate Chasselas-Pinot Blanc-Pinot Gris 2017
BC VQA Okanagan Valley 12.5% alc. $$-$$$

Chasselas is a grape variety rarely grown in Canada but the most widely planted variety in Switzerland. Here it adds to white pinots to make a very attractive wine with plenty of flavour, good weight, and lively acidity. The fruit is complex and defined and the overall balance is very good. You can pair this with poultry dishes of many kinds.

Quails' Gate Chenin Blanc 2017
BC VQA Okanagan Valley 13% alc. $$-$$$

This is a lovely, fresh chenin blanc that shows quality across the board. Look for bright, layered flavours, a little weight to the texture, and a very attractive seam of lively acidity. It's a very drinkable chenin that you can enjoy on its own, as an aperitif, and with white fish, seafood, and poultry.

Quails' Gate Dry Riesling 2017
BC VQA Okanagan Valley 12.5% alc. $$

This is a lovely, fresh-flavoured and textured riesling that's a real pleasure to drink on its own or with food. You can easily pair it with seafood (including smoked salmon and steamed mussels), white fish, and poultry. The fruit is bright and layered and it's supported by a broad seam of vibrant acidity. This is a well-balanced wine that's attractive and serious, and above all very drinkable.

Quails' Gate Gewürztraminer 2017
BC VQA Okanagan Valley 12.5% alc. $$

This is a beautiful, dry gewürztraminer made in a style that's far from the richly flavoured and somewhat viscous style common to Alsace. There's certainly some weight in the texture here, and it complements the well-defined fruit of the flavours, but this is a far more versatile style. It pairs well with slightly spicy food, but goes equally well with not-so-spicy white meat, fish, and seafood, as well as with slightly spicy lentil salads.

Quails' Gate' Stewart Family Reserve' Chardonnay 2016
BC VQA Okanagan Valley 13.5% alc. $$$

This is a fine chardonnay that shows how oak can enhance fruit without interfering with its purity. The flavours are fresh, focused, and well layered, and the acidity is balanced bright and clean. It's a pleasure to drink but it really needs food, and I suggest roasted chicken or turkey, veal and pork, and grilled white fish, all well seasoned because this chardonnay has the weight.

Road 13 Stemwinder 2015
BC VQA British Columbia 14% alc. $$

This is a blend of four white varieties: chardonnay (48%), viognier (39%), marsanne (9%), and roussanne (4%). It's an attractive wine for its flavours and texture. In terms of flavour it's marked by spicy fruitiness, while the texture is round and somewhat fleshy, with a good seam of fresh acidity. This is versatile with canapes and goes well with spicy chicken and seafood dishes.

Road 13 'Honest John's' White 2017
BC VQA British Columbia 13.3% alc. $$

Six grape varieties contributed their talents to this wine. Chardonnay (57%) and pinot gris (27%) starred in the leading roles, while chenin blanc, kerner, viognier, and orange muscat played cameos. They all add up to 100% and to a delicious white with focused, spicy fruit flavours backed by lovely, fresh acidity. This is a terrific mouthful you can enjoy on its own and with many chicken and seafood dishes, especially if they're somewhat spicy.

Benjamin Bridge Tidal Bay 2016
Nova Scotia 9.5% alc. $$

Blended from some of the winter-hardy grape varieties that grow in Nova Scotia, this is a very crisp white that goes well with the province's signature fish and seafood. The acidity is bright and vibrant, while the fruit is fresh and focused. Think of it for freshly shucked oysters and for grilled white fish with a squeeze of lemon.

Jost L'Acadie Chardonnay 2016
Nova Scotia 11.5% alc. $$

This is an off-dry blend of l'acadie blanc (a grape variety widely planted in Nova Scotia) and the much better-known chardonnay. The result is a light-to-medium-bodied white that's quite fruity and very easy-drinking. The fruit has good complexity and it's supported by bright, crisp acidity that contributes freshness to the texture. Enjoy it with sushi.

Jost L'Acadie Pinot Grigio 2016
Nova Scotia 12% alc. $$

This blend is primarily l'acadie blanc (a variety widely planted in Nova Scotia) with a little pinot grigio and it's slightly off-dry in style. The flavours combine herbal and fruit, and they're well balanced by a seam of fresh, clean acidity. It's medium weight and refreshing, the kind of wine you can sip on its own or pair with spicy food, including many Thai and Chinese dishes that feature vegetables, fish, chicken, or pork.

Jost Tidal Bay 2017
Nova Scotia 11% alc. $$

Tidal Bay is a category of wines made from specified grape varieties in Nova Scotia. The aim is to provide wines that are light, aromatic, and flavourful, and that go well with Nova Scotia's signature seafood-based cuisine. Jost's is a lovely example, with fruit-filled aromas and bright flavours that are balanced by clean, well-calibrated acidity. Naturally, it goes well with white fish and seafood.

CANADA—ONTARIO

Arterra Chardonnay 2016
VQA Niagara Peninsula 13.5% alc. $$$

This fine chardonnay is a natural for dishes such as lightly smoked fish or chicken, roast chicken, grilled salmon, and medium-strength cheeses. The fruit is concentrated and well-defined with a light veneer of sweet oak that enhances the fruit beautifully. The spine of acidity is clean and fresh, and the structure is detailed. This is a harmonious wine, a perfect example of the sum being far more that the totality of the parts, no matter how good the components are in this case.

Cave Spring Chardonnay 2016
VQA Niagara Escarpment 13.5% alc. $$-$$$

There's a lot of flavour in this chardonnay from one of Niagara Peninsula's most reliable producers. Look for complexity and decent structure in the fruit, along with an attractive hint of oak that enhances it, and bright, refreshing acidity. The wine is very well balanced and it's an excellent complement to grilled and roasted chicken, grilled white fish, and mild-to-medium-flavoured cheeses.

Cave Spring Chardonnay Musqué 2016
VQA Beamsville Bench 13.5% alc. $$

Chardonnay musqué is a variant of chardonnay that gives the wine—as you might expect from the name—a musky aroma and flavour. Not widely grown, it's sometimes added to white blends to give them some spiciness. This example is just lovely, with lightly spicy flavours supported by fresh, clean acidity to make for excellent balance. Enjoy it with lightly spiced or seasoned pork, chicken, seafood, and vegetable dishes.

Cave Spring CSV Riesling 2016
VQA Beamsville Bench 12% $$$

This is Cave Spring's top riesling, and it delivers exceptional quality, vintage after vintage. It's made in an off-dry style, but don't be put off if your preference is for dry wines. This one moves the needle only slightly, and any sweetness is well balanced by the bright acidity. The flavours are fresh and vibrant, and the wine is harmonious. Enjoy it with spicy seafood and pork dishes.

Cave Spring Estate Riesling 2016
VQA Beamsville Bench, Ontario 12% $$-$$$

Cave Spring Cellars focused on riesling from the beginning, and it's still the source of many of Niagara's finest rieslings—no mean feat, because the variety is one of the region's top performers and there are now scores of producers. Look for quite luscious fruit in this one, drawn from Cave Spring's Beamsville Bench vineyards. It's supported by refreshing, zesty acidity, giving the wine excellent balance. Drink it with seafood and white fish.

CANADA—ONTARIO

Cave Spring Cellars is one of the older family-owned wineries in Niagara Peninsula. Founded by the Pennachetti family and long-time winemaker Angelo Pavan, it quickly carved out a reputation as a producer of high-quality rieslings. Despite the opening of many other wineries making riesling—one of the grape varieties most suited to the growing conditions in Niagara—Cave Spring has retained its status as one of the region's notable producers of the variety. That said, many of Cave Spring's other wines are also first class, and their Blanc de Blancs sparkling wine is one of the finest fizzes in the region.

OKANAGAN VALLEY, BRITISH COLUMBIA, CANADA

Cave Spring Riesling 2016
VQA Niagara Peninsula, Ontario 11.5% alc. $$

Made in a lightly off-dry style, this is a wine that swings both ways. You can treat it as you would a wine with a touch of sweetness, and pair it with slightly spicy food, or treat it as a dry wine. You can just as easily drink it on its own or as an aperitif. Talk about versatile! The flavours are clean, bright, well focused and nicely complex, while the acidity is fresh and juicy.

Cave Spring Dry Riesling 2016
VQA Niagara Peninsula, Ontario 12% alc. $$-$$$

Cave Spring made its name with riesling and riesling continues to open doors for the company. This dry example opens with lovely citrus notes and continues to well-layered flavours. The acidity is bright and positive, never harsh, and the fruit-acid balance is right-on. Enjoy it with seafood, fish, and poultry.

Château des Charmes Aligoté 2017
VQA Niagara-on-the-Lake 12.5% alc. $$

Aligoté is a white grape variety widely planted in Burgundy and it's the classic white wine used (with crème de cassis) to make kir. Château des Charmes is one of the few Canadian wineries to make wine from it, and you'll find this example very attractive. It's crisp-textured and dry, and has well-defined fruit, well-balanced acidity, and very good integration. Drink it with chicken dishes of all kinds, with white fish, and with seafood.

Château des Charmes Riesling 2017
VQA Niagara-on-the-Lake 10.5% alc. $$

Only just slightly off-dry, you can pair this fine wine beautifully with many spicy Thai and Vietnamese dishes. The flavours are bright and serious, with plenty of complexity, and the acidity is vibrant. It's a delicious wine in its own right and so versatile that you can drink it on its own or as an aperitif, or take it to the table.

Château des Charmes Sauvignon Blanc 2017
VQA Niagara-on-the-Lake 12.5% alc. $$

This lovely sauvignon blanc, from one of Niagara Peninsula's reliable producers, delivers a quite nuanced flavour profile with fruit that's positive but nowhere near as powerful as sauvignons from, say, New Zealand. The acidity is crisp and balanced, and the wine is very attractive overall. Drink it with the usual suspects: white fish and seafood. But it's also very good with chicken and with not-too-spicy curries of chicken, pork, and tofu.

Fielding Pinot Grigio 2017
VQA Niagara Peninsula 12% alc. $$

This is a lovely dry pinot grigio that's a terrific partner for many dishes made with chicken or pork—roasts of either, as well as meats prepared in a creamy sauce. As for the wine, the fruit is quite concentrated and positive, with nice layering, and it's well balanced with crisp acidity. Overall, it's a very attractive wine that you can also drink on its own.

Fielding Riesling 2016
VQA Niagara Peninsula 11% alc. $$

Made in an off-dry style, this is a lovely riesling that shows an array of bright flavours. The fruit is underpinned by zesty acidity that cuts through the moderate sweetness, leaving you with just the right degree so that this wine is a perfect match for many slightly spicy dishes in the various south-east Asian traditions. Think of Thai and Vietnamese dishes with fish, seafood, chicken, pork, or tofu.

Flat Rock Riesling 2016
VQA Twenty Mile Bench 11% alc. $$

This is a fine riesling that's made in a slightly off-dry style that makes it perfect for drinking on its own, as an aperitif, or with slightly spicy dishes in Thai or other Asian cuisines. Look for lots of complexity in the bright flavours and for zesty acidity that helps to dry out the texture. Note some juiciness here, too, which is a bonus.

Henry of Pelham Chardonnay 2016
VQA Niagara Peninsula 11.5% alc. $$

This is a well-made chardonnay in a mid-range style. It delivers lovely, quite nuanced flavours that are consistent from start to finish, supported by a broad seam of fresh acidity. It's a balanced, attractive chardonnay that's very versatile with food. You can drink it with white meats, poultry, and white fish, with salads of many kinds, and with mild- to medium-strength cheeses.

Henry of Pelham Pinot Grigio 2017
VQA Niagara Peninsula 12.5% alc. $$

This is an easy-drinking, dry and fruity pinot grigio that you can enjoy on its own or drink with many chicken and pork dishes. The fruit is forward, with nice but not complicated layering, and the acidity is bright, clean, and well tailored to the fruit. It's a straightforward pinot grigio that makes a nice change from entry-level chardonnays if you're looking for a well-priced and versatile white wine.

Henry of Pelham Riesling 2016
VQA Niagara Peninsula 11.5% alc. $$

This is ever-so-slightly off-dry—a great place to be because you can think of it as either dry or off-dry. The flavours are deliciously fruity but in a fairly restrained way, and the acidity shines through brightly. All the components hold together very well, and you can enjoy this wine with many different foods: grilled or smoked white fish, poultry, pork, seafood, and summer salads, among them. Or you can simply sip it on its own.

Henry of Pelham Sauvignon Blanc 2016
VQA Niagara Peninsula 12.5% alc.　　　　　　　**$$**

Sauvignon blanc can be a tricky grape variety to grow in Niagara Peninsula because it's very sensitive to cold weather. But it does well in protected locations and produces some very fine wines. This example from Henry of Pelham shows lovely fresh fruit flavours. The acidity is broad and gentle but it effectively adds crispness to the texture. This is a sauvignon that goes very well with white fish, poultry, and seafood salads.

House Wine White 2016
VQA Ontario 11.5% alc.　　　　　　　**$$**

If you're looking for a well-priced wine to go with Thai or Vietnamese dishes, think of this one, made by the reliable people at Niagara Peninsula's Henry of Pelham winery. It's a blend of vidal and moscato grapes, with the latter dominating the flavours with its characteristic pungent flavours. Even so, it's not at all heavy or perfumed, but light on its feet, and it's dry and above all refreshing—just what you want with spicy food.

Jackson-Triggs Grand Reserve Niagara Estate Chardonnay 2016
VQA Niagara Peninsula 13.5% alc.　　　　　　　**$$$**

This is a dry, fruit-filled chardonnay that carries a fair bit of weight, but is far from overwhelming. The fruit is broad and concentrated, with plenty of complexity, and it's underpinned by clean acidity. The oak (from 6 months in barrel) is fairly prominent on the nose and a little less so in the flavours, and it will diminish over time. Enjoy it with smoked fish and meats.

Jackson-Triggs Grand Reserve Pinot Grigio 2016
VQA Niagara Peninsula 13% alc.   **$$-$$$**

This is a really attractive pinot grigio, a treat among the masses of mediocre pinot grigios on the market. It shows lovely flavours that are focused and a little spicy, and the support of a seam of fresh acidity that sets it up for food. You can enjoy this with many dishes, from poultry and pork to white fish and oysters—especially if you eat your oysters with a spicy condiment.

Lighthouse Riesling 2017
VQA Ontario 12.5% alc.   **$$**

The bright acidity in this essentially dry riesling, together with its fruitiness, makes it perfect for drinking on its own. Although fairly straightforward, there's some complexity to the flavours and the fruit-acid balance easily tilts it to food, too. If that's the way you go, it pairs well with slightly spicy or not-so-spicy dishes of all kinds fish, seafood, white meat, and vegetarian.

Malivoire Chardonnay 2016
VQA Beamsville Bench 13% alc.   **$$**

The Beamsville Bench, on the Niagara Peninsula, is a prime grape-growing site and this chardonnay shows the quality of many wines from the district. The lovely flavours are layered and nuanced and they're supported by well-calibrated acidity that contributes some very attractive juiciness to the texture. Dry and medium-bodied, this is a great choice for many chicken and pork dishes, as well as for white fish and mild cheeses.

Pillitteri 'Fusion' Gewürztraminer-Riesling 2017
VQA Niagara-on-the-Lake 12% alc. $$

The label says this is Medium-Dry, which sounds sweeter than off-dry, but this is not at all sweet. The flavours are dominated by the pungent notes of gewürztraminer (which makes up most of the blend) but the acidity of the riesling shines through clearly. It's well balanced and a very good pairing with many not-too-hot Asian dishes.

Red Stone 'Redfoot Vineyard' Viognier 2016
VQA Lincoln Lakeshore 13% alc. $$

Look for complexity and finesse in this lovely viognier. It's dry and packed with layers of fruit for a fairly big, mouth-filling texture. Everything's in balance here, with the rich fruit complemented by clean, well-calibrated acidity. This is a viognier that goes well with spicy food from one of the south-east Asian cuisines, such as Thai and Vietnamese.

Sibling Rivalry White 2016
VQA Niagara Peninsula 12% alc. $$

This is a blend made from riesling, chardonnay, and gewürztraminer. It makes for a very attractive, bright, and fruity white with quite concentrated flavours that run right through the palate. The acidity is well calibrated. This is an easy-drinking white you can sip on its own or pair with lightly spicy chicken, seafood, and vegetarian dishes.

Southbrook 'Connect' White Organic White 2017
VQA Ontario 11% alc. $$

This is a lovely white blend made from vidal, riesling, and chardonnay musqué. As you might expect, it has a little fruitiness and spiciness, and the flavours are pitched just right—not too intense and in your face, but not at all understated. The acidity is perfectly balanced. Drink this on its own or pair it with not-too-hot spicy dishes of seafood, chicken, or tofu.

Southbrook 'Triomphe' Chardonnay 2015
VQA Niagara Peninsula 12% alc. $$$

Originally located north of Toronto, Southbrook is now firmly situated on Niagara Peninsula, where it is one of the leading wineries in terms of environmentally sensitive production. This is a lovely chardonnay that shows myriad flavours, some weight to the texture, and fresh, clean acidity. It's perfectly balanced and harmonious, and goes very well with roast or grilled poultry and pork.

Sprucewood Shores Riesling 2016
VQA Ontario 12% alc. $$

Sprucewood Shores is located on the north shore of Lake Erie, in the Ontario appellation that goes by that name. This is a lovely off-dry riesling, with very attractive flavours in the focused and defined fruit, all balanced by crisp and clean acidity. It's a pleasure to drink on its own and it goes exceptionally well with slight spicy dishes (think some Asian cuisines) that feature seafood, poultry, and vegetables.

Sue Ann Staff Fancy Farm Girl 'Frivolous' White 2016
VQA Niagara Peninsula 11.5% alc. $$

This white blend clearly includes some riesling as it shows hints of the 'diesel' notes that are sometimes found in the aromas of that variety. Overall, this is a flavourful blend with crisp acidity that gives the texture some juiciness. It's essentially dry and goes well with many white fish and poultry dishes.

Tawse Riesling 2016
VQA Niagara Peninsula 10% alc. $$$

The Tawse winery is an impressive, gravity-fed structure, where the grapes arrive at the top and are processed on successively lower levels, with the barrel-room on the lowest. No pumping required. The care taken with the design is reflected in the wines, as in this lovely, bright, refreshing riesling. It has complexity and verve, with excellent balance. And it's an excellent pairing with many seafood and poultry dishes.

Tawse Unoaked Chardonnay 2017
VQA Niagara Peninsula 12.5% alc. $$$

Most chardonnays spend some time in contact with oak—in oak barrels, in stainless steel tanks with oak planks suspended in the wine, or with oak chips. But many, like this one, are unoaked, and it's a style preferred by many people. Here you'll find pure fruit flavours with very good complexity, supported by clean, refreshing acidity. It's dry and medium-bodied and a very good wine for poultry, pork, and white fish.

Thirty Bench 'Winemaker's Blend' Riesling 2016
VQA Niagara Peninsula 10.8% alc. $$$

Made in an off-dry style, this is a fine and luscious riesling that goes very well with slightly spicy dishes. Think of it next time you're cooking (or ordering) Thai food. The flavours of the wine are rich, layered, and structured, and the acidity is bright and vibrant so that it cuts through much of the potential sweetness. You can also, of course, enjoy this lovely wine on its own.

Trius Sauvignon Blanc 2016
VQA Niagara Peninsula 13.1% alc. $$

Niagara Peninsula can be a bit dodgy for growers of sauvignon blanc as it's sensitive to cold, yet the region turns out some excellent examples from vines planted in carefully selected locations. This one from Trius is really lovely. It has fresh, nuanced flavours that are perfectly balanced with crisp acidity, making it ideal to pair with food. Think of oysters and other shellfish, seafood, and white fish.

Casillero del Diablo Sauvignon Blanc 2017
Chile 13% alc. $$

This is a sauvignon blanc in the style that's become associated with New Zealand. You'll find that the flavours are concentrated with a touch of attractive sweetness to the fruit, with acidity that's zesty and bright. It's well balanced and all set to go to your table. You can't go wrong pouring this with seafood and white fish, and it will pair nicely with many poultry dishes, too.

Cono Sur 'Bicicleta' Pinot Grigio 2017
Chile 13.5% alc. $$

This is a well-balanced pinot grigio with crisp acidity that very effectively complements the fruit flavours. They, in turn, are bright and consistent from start to finish. The overall effect is a drinkable wine you can treat as casually as you like. Sip it on its own or pair it with chicken, turkey, and pork dishes. There's a little fruitiness that would suit slightly spicy foods, too.

CHILE

Cono Sur is best-known for its 'Bicicleta' series of affordable wines. The labels feature a bicycle and the brand is a nod to the bicycles the winery's workers use to get to and from work each day. Visitors to the winery are sometimes provided with bicycles to tour the Cono Sur vineyards. The bicycle is also a good symbol of Cono Sur's commitment to environmentally sensitive viticulture and winemaking. It was one of Chile's leaders in promoting non-chemical methods of dealing with vineyard problems—for example, using geese to control some pests. Cono Sur's 'Bicicleta' wines include an excellent viognier and pinot noir.

Cono Sur 'Bicicleta' Viognier 2017
Chile 13.5% alc.   **$$**

This is a really lovely wine for the price—it's long been one of the great bargain whites in Canada. It's easily recognizable as a viognier and beyond that delivers on all points. The flavours are nicely concentrated without being in your face, the acidity is fresh, and the texture is bright and clean. You can drink this with many dishes and it goes especially well with slightly spicy fish, pork, and chicken dishes.

Cono Sur Chardonnay 2017
Chile 13% alc.   **$$**

This chardonnay is made from organically grown grapes and the whole process (according to the label) is carbon-neutral. So it's a wine that will satisfy your green instincts. It'll satisfy your palate, too. It's full of concentrated and bright fruit flavours that are well balanced by refreshing acidity. It's fruit-driven and a chardonnay in a New World style, but there's no evident oak. Drink this on its own or with richer poultry and pork dishes, such as a well-seasoned pork roast or herbed chicken.

Emiliana 'Novas' Gran Reserva Sauvignon Blanc 2017
DO Valle de San Antonio 13.5% alc.   **$$**

The San Antonio Valley is located close to Chile's coast, where it benefits from the cold winds blowing off the Pacific Ocean. (The water is very cold in that region, thanks to a current running north from Antarctica.) The coolness promotes the bright, zesty acidity you can taste in the wine. It complements the lovely, fresh flavours of the wine and sets it up for food. Enjoy this with seafood and white fish.

Santa Rita Estate Reserve Sauvignon Blanc 2017
DO Valle de Casablanca 13.5% alc. $$

The Casablanca Valley, where the grapes for this wine grew, is only a few kilometres from the Pacific Ocean, and the cold winds off the water cool vineyards in the valley every day. The result is bright acidity in the grapes and the wine. That's perfect for sauvignon blanc, where you want a crisp texture. Here it complements the quite concentrated and focused flavours very well. Drink this with shellfish, seafood, and white fish. It's great with fish and chips.

Santa Rita Reserva Especial 120 Sauvignon Blanc 2017
DO Valle Central 13.5% alc. $$

From the long, broad Central Valley, this is a well-priced and well-made sauvignon blanc that goes well with seafood, white fish, chicken, and mild chicken, pork, or tofu curries. Look for fairly concentrated flavours with decent complexity and acidity that's well balanced. It's an affordable wine that's a good choice when you're having friends for a barbecue.

Viña Chocolan Chardonnay Reserva 2016
DO Valle del Maipo 13.5% alc. $$

The Maipo Valley is best known for cabernet sauvignon, but other varieties grow there, too. This well-made, balanced chardonnay is fresh and bright, the sort of wine you can drink on its own or pair with food—in this case you might think of roasted or grilled poultry and mild cheeses. The aromas, which show a little oak, are very attractive, while the nicely complex fruit flavours are supported by a seam of fresh, lively acidity.

Albert Bichot Chablis 2015
AOC Chablis 12.5% alc. $$$

Even the chardonnay-averse usually rally to Chablis—even though it's 100% the variety they profess to dislike. This one, from Albert Bichot, delivers restrained but fairly concentrated and very well-defined flavours. The acidity is spot-on for the fruit, and the texture is round and fresh. It's an easy wine to pair with fish, seafood, and fish soup (bouillabaisse would be excellent).

Bouchard Père & Fils Mâcon-Lugny Saint-Pierre 2016
AOC Mâcon-Lugny 12.5% alc. $$-$$$

This wine comes from a designated district in the Mâcon region of southern Burgundy. Made from char-donnay, it's an elegant wine that delivers nicely concentrated flavours that are well-defined and stylish. The texture is quite rich, with a little creaminess, while a seam of crisp acidity makes it refreshing. This is an excellent white for grilled salmon and for many white meat dishes.

Bouchard Père & Fils Petit Chablis 2016
AOC Petit Chablis 12% alc. $$$

Petit Chablis is one of the appellations in Burgundy's broader Chablis region and it's too often overlooked, perhaps because of its low minimum alcohol requirement. But with many people looking for lower alcohol levels in wine, this might be an ideal wine to go to. The flavours are restrained but positive, focused and well defined. The acidity makes it refreshing and adds some juiciness, and this is a great choice for seafood, shellfish, and white fish.

Bouchard Père & Fils Pouilly-Fuissé 2016
AOC Pouilly-Fuissé 13% alc. $$$$

Pouilly-Fuissé is a region in Burgundy famous for its white wines made from chardonnay. But don't expect to see this labelled as chardonnay, because it's the regional name that has all the cachet. This example is gorgeous and stylish, with pure and nuanced flavours and a smooth and fresh texture. Medium weight and dry, it's a great choice for seafood, fish, poultry, and pork dishes.

Château de Cléray Muscadet 2016
AOC Muscadet Sèvre et Maine Sur Lie 12% alc. $$

Muscadet, an appellation on the Loire River near the Atlantic Ocean, makes France's go-to wine for seafood. This example, from the Sauvion family, is an excellent pairing for oysters, mussels, and shrimp, as well as for white fish in general. Look for slightly aromatic flavours that are clean and fresh, crisp acidity, and some juiciness on the texture.

Coté Mas Blanc Mediterranée 2016
IGP Pays d'Oc 12.5% alc. $$

This is a four-way blend of grenache blanc and vermentino with a little sauvignon blanc and chardonnay for good measure. It's an unusual combination but it really works. This is a refreshing, drinkable white with bright fruit flavours and crisp, clean acidity. Drink it on its own or enjoy it with a salade niçoise, grilled calamari, or fish and chips.

Domaine Laroche 'Saint Martin' Chablis 2016
AOC Chablis 12% alc $$$

Saint Martin is a saint associated in France with wine, and Chablis is a premium region of Burgundy that's noted for its fine chardonnays—almost all made in stainless steel, rather than oak. Domaine Laroche is a notable producer, and this example shows lovely nuanced and layered fruit flavours combined with fresh, clean acidity. Balance is the keyword of the wine. Enjoy it with seafood, white fish, and poultry.

Fumées Blanches Sauvignon Blanc 2016
Vin de France 11.5% alc. $$

Made by the respected François Lurton, this is sauvignon blanc in a lighter style—light years, you might say, from the ever-popular Marlborough style. It shows good flavours and well-balanced, bright acidity, and it's an excellent choice for lighter dishes such as salads, white fish, seafood, and many chicken dishes.

Guy Saget Sancerre 2016
AOC Sancerre 13% alc. $$$$

White wines from the Sancerre region (in the Loire Valley) are made from sauvignon blanc, but don't think of New Zealand sauvignon blanc when you pick this bottle up. Sancerre is much more restrained than the typical New Zealand 'savvy', although the fundamentals are the same. With clean, fresh acidity, this is a great choice for white fish and seafood, as well as for many chicken dishes.

Jaffelin Bourgogne Aligoté 2016
AOC Bourgogne Aligoté 12.5% alc. $$

Aligoté, the white wine used (with crème de cassis) to make kir, is an underappreciated white variety. It's in the shadow of chardonnay in Burgundy, but makes a very good white with well-focused flavours and crisp acidity. This attractive example from Jaffelin goes very well with mild cheeses as well as with seafood, white fish, and chicken.

Les Dauphins Reserve Côtes du Rhône Blanc 2015
AOC Côtes du Rhône 13% alc. $$

This is a blend that's about two-thirds grenache blanc, complemented with marsanne, clairette, and viognier. There's a slight greenish tint to the light yellow colour, and the wine comes across as fresh and flavourful. The flavours are attractive and well measured, and the acidity is nicely calibrated and clean. This is an excellent choice for poultry and pork, as well as white fish, many vegetable dishes, and mild to medium flavoured cheeses.

Les Jamelles Sauvignon Blanc 2016
IGP Pays d'Oc 12% alc. $$

From the south of France, where you might think it's a little too warm to grow sauvignon blanc, comes this refreshing, somewhat aromatic example. It offers fresh fruit flavours with decent complexity, and a dose of vibrant acidity. It's well balanced and a wine you can sip on its own or drink with food. If you go the latter route, think of seafood and white fish dishes, including mussels in a white wine and garlic sauce or fish and chips.

Louis Bernard Côtes du Rhône Blanc 2016
AOP Côtes du Rhône 12.5% alc. $$

Most wines from the Côtes du Rhône region, in the south of the Rhône Valley, are red, and it's always a pleasure to come across a white. This one is mainly grenache blanc, viognier, and roussanne, and it strikes a lovely balance of focused fruit and fresh acidity. You can sip it on its own or pair it with poultry, pork, and even some slightly spicy dishes.

Louis Latour Bourgogne Chardonnay 2016
AOC Bourgogne 13% alc. $$$

For decades the producers of Burgundy didn't bother showing 'chardonnay' on the labels of their white wines, as almost all of them were. They do so now as a concession to consumers who buy by variety rather than region. This is a reliable chardonnay, vintage after vintage. It delivers concentrated and decently complex flavours and balanced, fresh acidity. You can't go wrong with this if you're serving poultry and white fish.

Thierry Delaunay Sauvignon Blanc 2016
AOP Touraine 12.5% alc. $$

Touraine is in the Loire Valley, in northern France, a cool wine area where sauvignon blanc does very well. This is a very attractive example, with lovely fruit that's positive but not at all over the top like so many New World sauvignons. It has crisp, well-balanced acidity, and a refreshing texture. Drink it with freshwater or ocean fish and seafoods of all kind, as well as with salads and chicken dishes.

Villa Blanche Chardonnay 2016
IGP Pays d'Oc 13.5% alc. $$

The Pays d'Oc region in the south of France produces a lot of good value wines. It's a generally warm region not far from the Mediterranean, and in summer the sea of green vines that cover the plains and hills provides a nice counterpoint to the blue water. This chardonnay sums it up nicely, with concentrated ripe fruit flavours that show some complexity, backed by well-tailored crisp acidity. It's a natural for chicken and fish and for summer salads.

Vive la Vie! Colombard-Gros Manseng 2016
Vin de France 11% alc. $$

"Vin de France" means that the grapes for the wine can be sourced from many different regions in the country. It doesn't denote high quality but many of these wines are very good. This is made in a popular fruity style, with quite concentrated flavours and crisp acidity. It is the sort of wine you can sip on its own, and it also goes well with slightly spicy dishes if they're not too heavy. Think of chicken, seafood, and pork.

Willm Réserve Riesling 2016
AOC Alsace 12% alc. $$

Alsace is well known for its rieslings, and Willm makes some fine examples. This Réserve is dry but the excellent fruit character softens the texture. The balanced acidity is bright and fresh. Overall, it's a harmonious wine that's versatile at the table, where you can drink it with chicken, seafood, and sushi.

Willm Réserve Gewürztraminer 2016
AOC Alsace 13% alc. $$

This is gewürztraminer in the style often associated with Alsace: full of pungent, spicy aromas and flavours, a little sweetness, and a touch of viscosity in the texture. It's a very good example, with well-balanced acidity that brings the wine to life and sets it up for food. This style of wine is often recommended for many Asian cuisines, and for good reason, and I suggest pouring next to many classic Thai dishes.

Yvon Mau Sauvignon Blanc 2015
IGP Côte de Gascogne 12.5% alc. $$

[1.5-litre bottle] If you're suspicious of large formats (unless they're expensive, and then a 1.5-litre bottle is called a 'magnum'!) try this sauvignon blanc. It's not complicated but it's very attractive and drinkable, and perfect for a gathering. The fruit is consistent and readily identifiable as sauvignon and the acidity is bright and fresh. It's excellent with white fish and seafood, with salads, and with many chicken dishes.

Black Tower Rivaner 2016
Landwein Rhein 9.5% alc. $

Black Tower has been around for more than 50 years and it's still such a popular wine that it's Germany's most-exported. Made from the rivaner variety (also known as müller-thurgau), it's moderately sweet, has fruity flavours, and shows bright, zesty acidity. It's easy-drinking on its own if you like sweeter wines, and it also goes well with spicy dishes of pork, chicken, or tofu in a number of Asian cuisines.

Blue Nun 2017
Landwein Rhein 9.5% alc. $

A long-time best-seller (although scorned by many wine critics), this is a refreshing blend because of its bright, zesty acidity. The flavours are fruity and fairly light, and there's just a little sweetness. It doesn't have a strong flavour profile, but there's nothing not to like here. It's great for sipping on a hot day (low alcohol counts) and you can pair it with light foods such as salads and spicy seafoods and poultry.

Deinhard Dry Riesling 2016
Qualitätswein Rheinhessen 12% alc. $$

This is a well-priced dry riesling that's very drinkable. The flavours are positive and consistent and the acidity is bright but not so steely that you can't drink this wine on its own, if you want to. It's very well balanced and goes well with smoked salmon, oysters and other seafood. If you want to compare a dry and off-dry riesling, try this with Deinhard 'Green Label' Riesling (the next wine).

Deinhard 'Green Label' Riesling 2016
Qualitätswein Mosel 10% alc. $$

This is off-dry, but only just off-dry—although if you compare it with Deinhard Dry Riesling (the entry before this) you'll clearly see that it's not dry. There are very attractive ripe flavours here, and the acidity is bright and crisp. The hint of sweetness raises the possibility of drinking it with spicy (but not too hot) foods such as many Thai dishes.

GREECE
Apelia Moschofilero 2016
IGP Peloponnese12% alc. $$

[1-litre bottle] This is a straightforward, uncomplicated white made from one of Greece's better-known grape varieties. You can imagine enjoying this with grilled fish at a taverna in a small fishing-port on the Mediterranean or Aegean. It's fresh, fruity, and crisp, and it would be lovely there, and it can be just as lovely on your patio as a well-priced, all-purpose white.

Malamatina Retsina NV
Greece 11% alc. $

[500mL] Retsina is made by adding pine sap to the fermenting wine. It's a process that goes back thousands of years when sap was spread in ceramic jars to make them impermeable and used as a preservative. Now it's a flavouring that gives medicinal, piney notes to the wine. It's not loved by everyone, but this is a wine that goes well with olives, stuffed grape leaves, and grilled calamari.

HUNGARY

Chapel Hill Sauvignon Blanc NV
Hungary 12% alc. $$

Not from Chapel Hill in North Carolina (although they do make wine near there) this is a straightforward, uncomplicated sauvignon blanc from Hungary. It delivers quite vibrant fruit flavours backed by fresh, clean acidity. It's well balanced and is versatile at the table; drink it with white fish, seafood, and poultry, vegetarian salads, or with mild-flavoured cheeses

Dunavar Pinot Grigio 2017
IGP Felsö-Magyarország 11.5% alc. $

This is a very straightforward, very attractive, and very drinkable white that you can sip on its own or enjoy with casual meals such as a green salad, a chicken sandwich, mild cheese. It has quite concentrated flavours balanced by crisp, bright acidity. There's nothing complicated here, just a refreshing, flavourful white wine.

ITALY

Amatore Bianco Verona 2016
IGT Verona 12.5% alc. $

Made near Verona (remember Romeo and Juliet?), this is a blend of garganega, a local grape, sauvignon blanc, and other varieties. Whether the young star-cross'd lovers ever tasted it (there was no minimum drinking age then) isn't known, but it's an essentially dry and fruity wine, with a touch of sweetness at mid-palate. The acidity is good and crisp. You can drink this on its own or pair it with lightly spiced seafood and chicken.

Bollini Pinot Grigio 2016
DOC Trentino 13% alc. $$-$$$

This is a deservedly popular Italian pinot grigio. It stands out from the herd by having components that show quality in their own right and are balanced with one another. The fruit is quite rich and nuanced, with some lovely spicy notes, and it's complemented by fresh acidity. The texture is smooth and quite round. This is great for sipping on its own, and goes well with pasta in a cream sauce, seafood, whitefish, and chicken dishes.

Casal Thaulero Pinot Grigio 2017
IGP Terre di Chieti 13% alc. $

This wine comes from the Chieti district of Abruzzo, in central Italy. It's a fairly light-bodied pinot grigio that delivers uncomplicated flavours right through the palate. The fruit is backed by bright, crisp acidity. This is an easy choice if you're looking for a lighter, easy-drinking white to sip on its own or to drink with a chicken sandwich or fish burger.

Cesari 'Adesso' Chardonnay 2015
Italy 12% alc. $

Most of the Italian wine sold in Canada is from indigenous varieties such as sangiovese and primitivo, but Italy's vineyards include a lot of 'international' varieties, too. This is a very affordable chardonnay that does the trick across the board. The flavours are quite concentrated with some complexity and the acid is fresh and balanced. It's a wine that's easy to pair with mild cheeses, pork and chicken dishes.

Citra Pinot Grigio 2017
IGT Terre di Chieti 13% alc. $

The Citra brand delivers wines that are inexpensive and good quality. This pinot grigio is more attractive than many of its more expensive siblings because it's dry, has restrained fruit, and a nice level of crisp, clean acidity. It's refreshing drunk on its own, and an easy pairing with many foods, from a simple chicken sandwich to grilled white fish.

Concilio Pinot Grigio 2016
DOC Trentino 13% alc.   **$$**

This is a lighter style of pinot grigio that delivers defined but understated flavours. They're complemented by a spine of zesty, clean acidity that gives the wine a crisp, bright texture. It's well balanced and an easy choice if you're serving seafood, shellfish, or white fish.

Fantini 'Farnese' Pinot Grigio 2016
IGP Terre Siciliane 12% alc.   **$**

Look for good, fruity flavours and crisp acidity in this inexpensive and good quality pinot grigio from Sicily. It's dry, light-to-medium-bodied, refreshing, and easy-drinking —not too complicated but a very pleasant wine for drinking on its own or with food. Potential partners are fish and seafood, chicken and summer salads.

Folonari Pinot Grigio 2016
IGT delle Venezie 11.5% alc.   **$$**

This is a slightly lighter style of pinot grigio than many, and it shows attractive flavours and a seam of fresh acidity. It's dry and medium bodied, has some complexity in the fruit and a crisp texture. It's not a complicated wine, but it's very easy to drink. Sip it on its own or drink it with food, where you might think of lighter dishes such as salads, seafood, and roast chicken.

GRAPEVINE ARBOUR AT CONCHA Y TORO VINEYARD, SANTIAGO, CHILE

Gabbiano 'Promessa' Pinot Grigio 2016
IGT delle Venezie 12.5% alc. $$

This is a very attractive, quite delicate pinot grigio from a producer known for reliably quality wines. 'Quite delicate' doesn't mean flavourless or bland, but there's a real lightness of touch here that sets it apart from most of the Italian pinot grigios on the market. The fruit-acid balance is very good, and this is an excellent choice for many lighter foods such as seafood, white fish, and poultry.

Masi Masianco 2016
IGT delle Venezie 13% alc. $$

This is a lovely blend of pinot grigio and verduzzo, a little-known grape variety from the area around Venice, in north-east Italy. The wine is fresh and yet serious, with good, concentrated and complex fruit that sits in excellent balance with the fresh acidity. This is a terrific wine that goes with many kinds of food, from poultry and pork to salads and medium-strength cheeses.

Melini Orvieto Classico 2016
DOC Orvieto Classico 12.5% alc. $-$$

This wine is made around the town of Orvieto, a town so steeped in the history of wine that its medieval cathedral is adorned with images of vines. Made mainly from the grechetto and trebbiano varieties, this is an attractive and refreshing wine with layered fresh fruit flavours and crisp acidity. It's not a complicated wine, but it's terrific drinking, either on its own or with light foods such as salads and quiches.

Pasqua Pinot Grigio delle Venezie 2017
DOC Pinot Grigio delle Venezia 12% alc. $$

If you're looking for an easy-drinking wine with some quality, try this pinot grigio. It's slightly aromatic with very pleasant and attractive flavours through the palate, and the supporting acidity is crisp and clean. It's dry and light-medium in body, and it's very good to drink on its own. You can also drink it with light foods such as salads, roasted chicken, and sushi.

Ruffino 'Lumina' Pinot Grigio 2016
IGT delle Venezie 12% alc. $$

For the very affordable price, this is an elegant pinot grigio. The texture is smooth and mouth-filling, but it's also refreshing, thanks to the broad seam of acidity that underlies the well-defined and bright fruit. It's dry and medium-bodied, and it goes well with chicken, pork, pasta in a cream sauce, and mild cheeses.

Ruffino Orvieto Classico 2016
DOC Orvieto Classico 12% alc. $$

The label shows the façade of the cathedral in Orvieto, which glows gold as you look at the town across the vineyards that produced this wine. It's a lovely, well-balanced white that shows fresh, positive but somewhat understated fruit. The acidity is well-calibrated, making the wine refreshing and suitable for sipping on its own or for pairing with poultry, pork, fettuccine alfredo, and mild cheeses.

Santa Margherita Pinot Grigio 2016
DOC Valdadige 12.5% alc. $$

This is a very popular pinot grigio and for good reason. It's a well-made wine that shows a lot more complexity in the flavours than most, and it has excellent fruit-acid balance. The texture is bright and crisp, and there's some substance here, unlike the watery efforts that too often pass for pinot grigio. It's dry and medium bodied and you can drink it with many chicken and white fish dishes.

Kim Crawford Sauvignon Blanc 2017
Marlborough 12% alc. $$-$$$

Kim Crawford sauvignon blanc is an almost iconic wine that sells briskly everywhere. It's rich and complex in flavours that span a broad spectrum, and they're paired with acidity that's remarkably deep, broad, and zesty. It's a well-balanced wine that goes well with many foods, from freshly shucked oysters and other seafood to mild curries and goat cheese and tomato tart.

Matua's co-founder, Bill Spence, was the first person to plant sauvignon blanc in New Zealand. That was in 1969, and Matua produced its first sauvignon blanc in 1974—400 bottles of it. Bill could hardly have known how important it would be, as a couple of decades later sauvignon blanc became New Zealand's calling-card in the world of wine and now exports millions of bottles a year. Matua still makes fine sauvignon blancs from both the Hawkes Bay and Marlborough regions, as well as wines made from pinot noir, chardonnay, pinot gris, and merlot and from less common (to New Zealand) varieties such as albariño and malbec.

Matua Sauvignon Blanc 2017
Hawkes Bay 13% alc. $$

The great majority of New Zealand sauvignon blancs come from Marlborough, at the northern end of the South Island, but this is from Hawkes Bay, on the east coast of the North Island. The growing conditions there produce somewhat different flavours and generally softer texture, but you'll still find in this wine the clean acidity needed for a wine to pair well with food. Enjoy this sauvignon blanc with seafood and oysters, and with many curried dishes.

Nobilo Sauvignon Blanc 2017
Marlborough 12% alc. $$

This is a lovely, fresh Marlborough sauvignon blanc that lacks what's often referred to as the 'sweatiness' of many. Here the fruit is pure and clean, and it's complemented by the same sort of acidity: crisp, even zesty, and giving some juiciness to the texture of the wine. Overall, it's a very appealing style. Freshly shucked oysters go very well with this, as do other shellfish, seafoods, and white fish. Think of it when you're having fish and chips.

Oyster Bay Chardonnay 2016
Marlborough 13.5% alc. $$

Marlborough is known world-wide for sauvignon blanc, but in fact many varieties grow well in the region. This chardonnay shows a hint of oak in the aromas and flavours, but they're dominated by fresh fruit that is nicely focused and layered. The acidity is balanced and clean, and this makes an excellent choice for smoked fish, medium-strength cheeses, and many pork and chicken dishes.

Oyster Bay Pinot Grigio 2017
Hawkes Bay 12.5% alc. $$

Marlborough, New Zealand's best-known wine region because of its sauvignon blancs, is so dominant that it's sometimes a surprise to see a big-production wine from a different region—in this case Hawkes Bay, on the east coast of the North Island. This is an attractive, easy-drinking white with lovely flavours and bright acidity.

Oyster Bay Sauvignon Blanc 2017
Marlborough 12.5% alc. $$

There's an ocean of Marlborough sauvignon blanc (known in New Zealand as 'savvy') and although there's a certain consistent style, some stand apart. This one from Oyster Bay is much less in your face than many, and shows well-defined flavours and bright, clean acidity. The fruit-acid balance is very good, and this is a good choice for many white fish and seafood dishes.

Peter Yealands Sauvignon Blanc
Marlborough, 12.5% alc. $$

This is a fairly elegant sauvignon blanc that shows very attractive and quite complex fruit right through the palate. The bright, crisp acidity is well calibrated to the fruit and it adds some juiciness to the texture. Balance is the key to this wine, not only among the components but in its overall impression. It's definitely a food wine, and it goes very well with freshly shucked oysters, smoked salmon, and white fish of most kinds.

Riverlore Sauvignon Blanc 2017
Marlborough 13% alc. $$

There's plenty of bright, zesty acidity in this sauvignon blanc from New Zealand's premium source. The fruit is positive and it drives the wine, but it's not at all aggressive, as some sauvignon blancs can be, and it doesn't interfere with food it's paired well with. As for those foods, think of oysters and other shellfish and seafoods, white fish, and many chicken dishes.

Sacred Hill Sauvignon Blanc 2017
Marlborough 12.5% alc. $$-$$$

Sacred Hill is definitely a cut above most of the New Zealand sauvignon blancs (called 'savvies' in New Zealand) on the market. There's excellent balance between the focused, well-defined fruit flavours and the clean, crisp acidity. Clearly New World and fruit-driven, it's built for food. Suggested pairings include the usual savvy suspects: seafood and white fish, especially oysters.

Villa Maria Sauvignon Blanc 2017
Marlborough 12.5% alc. $$

This is classic Marlborough sauvignon blanc, made in the pungent, full-throated style that swept the world in the late 1990s and still has a major following. The fruit is intensely flavoured with good complexity and a sense of ripe-sweetness, and it's supported by bright, quite dense acidity. A little too much for oysters and delicate white fish, it goes well with many curried dishes featuring chicken and seafood.

White Cliff 'Winemaker's Selection'
Sauvignon Blanc 2017
Marlborough 12.5% alc. $$

This is a very well-balanced savvy (as sauvignon blanc is called in New Zealand), with bright and persistent flavours complemented by quite zesty acidity. There's some nice layering in the fruit, and the acid is very well balanced. Dry and medium bodied, this is a great choice for oysters and other shellfish, for white fish (and fish and chips), and for white meats generally.

Whitehaven Sauvignon Blanc 2017
Marlborough 13% alc. $$-$$$

Look for loads of flavour and complexity in this wine that the back label describes as a "quintessential Marlborough Sauvignon Blanc." It's no exaggeration, as this expresses the key flavours that are widely associated with the variety and place. The fruit is forward and very positive and the acidity is clean and assertive. Drink it with oysters and a spicy condiment, white fish and lemon, or mild- to medium-strength curries.

SOUTH AFRICA
Fleur du Cap Chardonnay 2016
WO Western Cape 13.5% alc. $$

This is a well-priced, versatile chardonnay that you can drink on its own or pair with many different foods. Poultry, salads, pork, white fish, and mild cheeses are only the first to spring to mind. Look for attractive, fresh flavours in this wine. There's some complexity and the fruit is effectively backed by clean, measured acidity.

Nederburg 'The Winemasters' Sauvignon Blanc 2017
WO Western Cape 13.5% alc. $$

This is a fresh sauvignon blanc that shows attractive, reasonably complex flavours with good concentration. The acidity is crisp and clean, and it lifts the fruit nicely. Unlike some over-the-top sauvignons, the fruit here is held in check, and the refreshing texture sets it up for food. White fish (and fish and chips) and seafood are no-brainers, as are warm goat cheese salad and goat cheese and tomato tart.

SPAIN

Honoro Vera 2016
DO Rueda 13% alc. $$

Look for very attractive fruity flavours with decent complexity, all underpinned by crisp acidity. It adds up to a straightforward, not too complicated white that's refreshing enough to drink on its own or to pair with food. If you're inclined to the latter, think of seafood and white fish, simple chicken dishes (such as roast chicken), and mild cheeses.

Liberado Verdejo-Sauvignon Blanc 2016
Vino de la Tierra de Castilla 12% alc. $$

This is a fruity, easy-drinking white from the sprawling Castilla region in central Spain. It's an attractive blend that brings together the freshness of sauvignon blanc and the complex flavours of verdejo. What you get is a white with solid and persistent flavours that are bright and clean, supported by crisp, well-balanced acidity. It goes really well with warm goat cheese salad, with fish and chips, and with many seafood dishes.

Marqués de Riscal Rueda 2017
DO Rueda 12.5% alc. $$

Made from the verdelo variety (verdejo in Spanish) this is a nicely made and very drinkable white. It delivers quite understated and well-sculpted flavours that are supported by a seam of brisk, clean acidity. Think of an old world sauvignon blanc in terms of style. It's a refreshing, crisp wine you can enjoy on its own or as an aperitif or as a partner for seafood and white fish.

USA—CALIFORNIA

Apothic 'Winemaker's Blend' White 2015
California 12.5% alc. $$

This is an off-dry white blend that delivers concentrated and nicely layered flavours. They lead the way, but the acidity is bright and fresh and balances the slight sweetness very effectively. The texture is round and mouth-filling. It's a refreshing wine you can easily drink on its own, and if you want to pair it with food you might look for chicken or pork that has been prepared with some spices in an Asian cuisine.

Beringer 'Founders' Estate' Chardonnay 2016
California 13.9% alc. $$

The founders referred to in the name are the Beringer brothers, who founded this winery in 1876. They couldn't have foreseen how big and prominent their business would be more than 140 years later. This chardonnay is well made and very satisfying, especially when paired with poultry, pork, and seafood. The flavours are bright and fresh, as is the well-balanced acidity. Overall, it's very attractive and easy-drinking.

Beringer 'Founders' Estate' Pinot Grigio 2016
California 13% alc. $$

As popular as pinot grigio is, and as maligned as chardonnay is, chardonnay is still the world's most popular white wine. Yet there's a massive amount of pinot grigio around, too much of it bland and characterless. This is far from that. You'll find quite concentrated and well-defined flavours here, with clean, bright acidity and very good balance. It's an easy choice if you're looking for a white wine to sip on its own or to accompany chicken, pork, or mild cheeses.

Beringer 'Founders' Estate' Sauvignon Blanc 2016
California 13.5% alc. $$

California wines have a reputation for weight and intensity, but in fact its wines come in many styles. This sauvignon blanc is more nuanced and understated than bold, but the flavours are still focused and well defined. The acidity is fresh and clean and in good balance to the fruit. You can drink it on its own or pair it with seafood and white fish, as well as with chicken and mild vegetable, chicken, and pork curries.

Beringer Napa Valley Chardonnay 2016
Napa Valley 14.5% alc. $$$

This is a big-bodied, luscious chardonnay that's perfect for rich white meat and seafood dishes, such as lobster with butter, scallops, and chicken or veal in a cream sauce. The flavours are rich, persistent and textured, with plenty of depth, and they're complemented by fresh acidity that gives the wine some juiciness—what's called a salivant character in France, because it sets you up for food.

Bonterra Chardonnay 2016
Mendocino County 13.3% alc. $$

This is made from organically farmed grapes, meaning that no chemicals were used in the vineyards (as pesticides or herbicides or to keep vine diseases at bay). It's characterized by pure fruit flavours with just a hint of oak in the flavours but more in the texture. It's bright and clean, with good acidity, and it's very balanced overall. This is a great chardonnay for chicken and pork dishes, as well as for white fish and mild cheeses such as camembert.

Canyon Road Chardonnay 2016
California 13% alc. $$

This is an entry-level, no-nonsense, straightforward chardonnay in a style that has many followers. The fruit is ripe-sweet (there's a little residual sugar here) and fruity and the acidity is on the low side. This means the texture is round, smooth, and mouth-filling. The low acidity means you have to be careful not to drink it with acidic foods, but most chicken and pork dishes are good bets.

Fetzer 'Sundial' Chardonnay 2016
Califiornia 13% alc. $$

The aromas and flavours of this mid-range chardonnay show a little toastiness from the oak-aging, but it's far from enough to interfere with the fruit flavours. There's nothing outstanding about this wine, but it's a well-priced entry-level chardonnay that's balanced and attractive. It goes well with simple dishes such as chicken or fish burgers.

Fetzer 'Shaly Loam' Gewürztraminer 2016
Monterey 12% alc. $$

This is an attractive and well-priced gewürztraminer made in an off-dry style. The flavours are quite rich and very varied, with a little of the muskiness often found in this variety. They're supported by fresh acidity that cuts through the slight sweetness and sets the wine up for food. Gewürztraminer is often suggested for spicy Asian cuisine, and this one's no exception. Try it with spicy Thai and Vietnamese dishes with seafood, pork, or tofu.

Franciscan Napa Valley Chardonnay 2015
Napa Valley 13.5% alc. $$$

Here's a beautiful richly flavoured and textured chardonnay that speaks with a California accent through and through. Don't think that means it's over-oaked—that's a cliché that's very misleading. There's a hint of oak here, but it adds complexity and enhances the texture. The fruit itself is complex and delicious. Overall this is a well-balanced chardonnay that's ideal with rich poultry, pork (and pork belly), and seafood (lobster, scallops).

J. Lohr 'Riverstone' Chardonnay 2016
Arroyo Seco, Monterey 13.5% alc. $$-$$$

This is a fairly opulent chardonnay that delivers rich flavours that are focused, layered, and well defined. The oak aging is evident but well managed and this is anything but an 'oaky chard'. The fruit is supported by well-calibrated acidity, which sets the wine up for food. This is a great choice for full-flavoured dishes featuring poultry and pork —think well-seasoned roasts—and it's an excellent partner for mild- or medium-flavoured cheeses.

Joseph Carr 'Josh' Chardonnay 2015
California 13.5% alc. $$-$$$

This is a rich, full-bodied chardonnay made in a sort of classic California way. It's fruit-driven, round and smooth, with plenty of luscious flavours. There's a little oak on the palate, but it adds complexity and is well managed. The acidity is fresh and clean, making this an excellent wine for many foods. I suggest richer seafood (such as lobster and scallops), poultry, and pork.

Kendall-Jackson 'Vintner's Reserve' Chardonnay 2016
California 13.5% alc. $$-$$$

This is a fruit-driven chardonnay with a rich, mouth-filling, soft texture. The fruit is concentrated and well-layered and the acidity, while not high, has a little bite to it—enough to make the wine suitable for the table. With flavours that are ripe-sweet, this is a good wine for roast chicken and turkey and also for the likes of butter chicken and chicken pad thai.

La Crema Monterey Chardonnay 2016
Monterey 13.5% alc. $$$

La Crema's chardonnays are consistently fine and elegant across vintages. This one shows well sculpted flavours that are layered and nuanced. They're complemented by fresh acidity that gives some juiciness to the texture and complements its slight creaminess. Enjoy this chardonnay with richer seafood (lobsters and scallops, for example), pastas in cream sauce, and with pork and chicken dishes.

Meiomi Chardonnay 2016
Monterey County, Sonoma County,
Santa Barbara County 13.9% alc. $$$

Look for rich, ripe-sweet flavours in this chardonnay, which comes packed with fruit. But it's not a mindless fruit-bomb (exploding with fruit at the expense of everything else). The acidity clicks in effectively to cut through the fruitiness, and there's some good structure to the wine. It's full-bodied, so serve it with substantial food. Rich fish dishes (prepared in cream sauces or with butter) are one way to go.

Murphy Goode Chardonnay 2015
California 13.5% alc. $$$

This is a lovely chardonnay that shows careful work with the barrels. The result is some attractive nuances to the flavour and texture, but this is anything but what's often called 'an oaky chard'. The flavours are dominated by fresh fruit and they're complemented by fresh acidity that gives the wine some juiciness. It's medium bodied and dry and goes well with chicken, pork, seafood, and white fish.

Pepperwood Grove Pinot Grigio 2017
California 12.5% alc. $$

This is a fairly substantial and dry pinot grigio. In terms of flavour, the fruit is concentrated and forward and dominated by notes that speak to the sweetness of ripe grapes rather than to residual sugar. The acidity is vibrant, clean, and well balanced, and it sets the wine up for food. This is a good pairing for grilled chicken and roasted turkey, and it will extend to many white fish and seafood dishes.

Raymond 'Family Classic' Chardonnay 2015
California 13.5% alc. $$

Here's a chardonnay that speaks with a California accent. Look for plush fruit in the full-bodied wine. There's plenty of complexity, a hint of oak in the flavours, and there's some weight and creaminess to the texture. At the same time, the acidity comes through bright and crisp. All the components hold together extremely well, and this is a great choice for poultry, pork, and richer seafoods, such as scallops and lobster.

Robert Mondavi 'Private Selection' Chardonnay 2016
California 13.5% alc. $$

This is a very attractive chardonnay that goes well with many foods. Think of it for poultry and pork, fish and seafood, and for cheeses that are quite mild in strength. In the wine you'll find plenty of flavours that are concentrated and well layered, along with fresh acidity and very good balance. All the components are well integrated, and this is a wine priced so that you can serve it on both casual and less casual occasions.

Robert Mondavi Fumé Blanc 2015
Napa Valley 13.5% alc. $$-$$$

Fumé Blanc is sauvignon blanc that's been fermented or aged in barrels, unlike most sauvignon blancs (such as most of those from New Zealand's Marlborough region) that are made entirely in stainless steel tanks. The oak gives wonderful depth to the sauvignon and enhances the flavours and texture. This is a terrific wine and it goes well with poultry and white fish (which could be smoked) as well as medium-strength cheeses.

Rodney Strong 'Charlotte's Home' Sauvignon Blanc 2015
Northern Sonoma/Sonoma County 13.5% alc. $$-$$$

Sauvignon blanc comes in many styles, from the powerful 'savvies' of New Zealand to the understated sauvignons of northern France. This California example finds a very happy place in the middle, where it has positive and concentrated flavours with the fresh acidity that sets it up for food. Dry, medium-bodied, and well balanced, it goes very well with white fish and seafood dishes.

Three Thieves Pinot Grigio 2016
California 13.5% alc. $$

This is a fruit-forward pinot grigio that has more textural weight than many. The flavours are solid, persistent, and reasonably complex, and the acidity clicks in to provide crispness and freshness. It's medium bodied and dry, and you can enjoy it on its own or with food. It goes well with roast chicken and turkey, many seafoods, and grilled white fish.

Tom Gore Chardonnay 2016
California 13.5% alc. $$-$$$

Contrary to the widespread notion that all California chardonnays are over-oaked, the great majority (that I've tasted, anyway) show very judicious use of barrels for fermentation and/or aging. This one is dominated by fresh fruit flavours that are long and deep and backed by fresh, clean acidity. It's a food-friendly chardonnay that goes well with chicken and pork in many forms, and with rich seafood such as scallops and lobster.

Tom Gore Sauvignon Blanc 2016
California 13.5% alc. $$-$$$

Sauvignon blanc might seem an odd variety to come out of California because it's generally grown in cooler areas. But California has a rich diversity of climatic conditions and can produce wines like this lovely, crisp-textured sauvignon. The flavours are positive and forward, but by no means over-the-top, and there's very good balance and structure. You can drink it on its own or with chicken, white fish, and seafood.

Wente 'Louis Mel' Sauvignon Blanc 2016
Livermore Valley San Francisco Bay 13% alc. $$-$$$

This is a very nice take on sauvignon blanc. It's not the blowsy, in-your-face style that's very popular and often associated with Marlborough (in New Zealand), but it shows restrained fruit that's well defined and quite complex. The acidity is well done: clean and bright and very approachable, and the overall balance is right-on. You can enjoy this with oysters and other shellfish and with seafood and white fish more generally.

Wente 'Morning Fog' Chardonnay 2016
Livermore Valley-San Francisco Bay 13.5% alc. $$-$$$

This is a weighty chardonnay that comes across with some lightness that makes it quite versatile with food. It shows concentrated and well-layered fruit that's fresh and bright, supported by clean, refreshing acidity. All the components are well balanced and the freshness sets it up for creamy textured dishes (think some white pastas), as well as chicken, turkey, pork, and weightier white fish dishes.

USA—WASHINGTON
Kung Fu Girl Riesling 2016
Columbia Valley $$

This is a very appealing riesling that lies in that food-versatile and deservedly popular space between dry and off-dry. That means you can serve it successfully with such dishes as roast chicken and smoked salmon, as well as Pad Thai and well-seasoned grilled pork. The flavours are bright, layered, and persistent and the acidity is clean, fresh, and juicy. Of course you can also drink this on its own, if you want to.

Wine makes daily living easier, less hurried, with fewer tensions and more tolerance.

– BENJAMIN FRANKLIN

RED WINES

ARGENTINA
Alamos Cabernet Sauvignon 2016
Mendoza 13% alc.   **$$**

Made by the Catena family, one of Argentina's famous wine families, this is a concentrated, well-structured cabernet sauvignon with excellent balance. It's readily identifiable as cabernet sauvignon, with solid, spicy fruit flavours that are backed by fresh, clean acidity. The tannins are easy-going and this is an excellent wine for grilled read meats and grilled vegetables.

Alamos Malbec 2016
Mendoza 13% alc.   **$$**

Malbec has become Argentina's signature red wine and this is a very good example in the affordable price bracket. It's very versatile with food, being fruit-driven yet very well balanced and with decent structure. Look for complexity in the flavours, freshness in the acidity, and for well-integrated tannins. It's an easy choice for red meats (what Argentines eat with their malbec) as well as with beef empanadas and burgers.

Argento 'Selección' Cabernet Sauvignon 2017
Argentina 13% alc. $$

This is a straightforward, well-priced cabernet sauvignon that's made in a light-to-medium-bodied style. The fruit is fresh and decently layered and it's supported by clean, fresh acidity, It's dry with easy-going tannins. You'll find this a versatile red that goes with many dishes, from burgers to steak, from mushroom pie to roast chicken.

Argento Reserva Cabernet Sauvignon 2015
Mendoza 13.5% alc. $$

Look for solid and concentrated flavours in this attractive cabernet sauvignon. They're very positive but not at all excessively intense and they're well complemented by fresh acidity. It's a dry wine that verges on astringent, and the tannins are still quite firm but manageable. Beef seems to be the daily dish in Argentina, so it's a safe bet that this cabernet will go well with steaks and other cuts of beef.

Argento 'Selección' Malbec 2017
Mendoza 13% alc. $$

The malbec grapes for this wine were grown in high altitude (that is, in the foothills of the Andes) in fairly cool conditions. Add plenty of sunlight and you get fruit that is ripe and holds a good level of acidity. Transfer those qualities to the wine, and you have a malbec that's fruity and fresh, and an excellent choice for food. It's not high in alcohol or over-bearing in weight, and goes well with red meats as well as many pork dishes.

Argento Reserva Malbec 2016
Mendoza 14% alc. $$

When the first Argentine malbecs started flowing to export markets they were the first wave of a veritable

ARGENTINA
Catena Zapata is one of Argentina's best-known and most-respected wineries. Located in the Uco Valley, in the sprawling Mendoza region, it is housed in a distinctive structure (La Pyramide) that evokes the architecture of the Inca people of northern South America. The winery was the brainchild of Nicolas Catena, and the most prominent member of the family is now Laura Catena, a physician and winemaker. Catena is especially known for wines made from the malbec variety, but it also grows and uses other varieties, and the Catena Institute does research on varieties and vine-growing locations in the Mendoza region.

tsunami. It's ebbed somewhat, but we're still awash with malbecs, some terrific, others very good, some mediocre. This is a well-priced, good-quality example that shows consistent and concentrated fruit and well-balanced, fresh acidity. The tannins are firm but approachable, and it's a good choice for red meats, grilled sausages, and burgers.

Bousquet Cabernet Sauvignon 2016
Tupungato Valley, Mendoza 13% alc. $$

Although Argentina is known for malbec, it also produces other excellent red (and white) wines. In this cabernet sauvignon you'll find lovely, well-managed flavours that are concentrated but far from the overwhelming fruit you sometimes find. Balance is the keyword for this cabernet, where all the components are well harmonized. The obvious food suggestion is beef, but this goes with all meats and any other food you feel like drinking red wine with.

Bousquet Malbec 2017
Tupungato Valley, Mendoza 13.5% alc. $$

This wine is made from organically grown grapes, so no chemicals were used in its production. The vineyard is in the foothills of the Andes (about 1200 metres above sea level) where cooler conditions promote acidity in the grapes. What you get is a very well-balanced malbec, with lovely fruit flavours supported by fresh acidity. Meanwhile, the tannins are soft and easy to deal with. This is an excellent wine for roasted red meats, and it also goes well with fairly strong cheeses.

Catena Cabernet Sauvignon 2015
Mendoza 13% alc. $$-$$$

The vineyards from which this wine was sourced are planted high in the foothills of the Andes, where they get a lot of sun during the day and experience cool temperatures at night. The variation produces grapes that are ripe with good acidity, and they translate these qualities to the wine. Look for concentrated, ripe flavours with impressive layering and structure, and the fresh acidity that makes the wine so suitable for food. With moderate tannins, it's an excellent choice for red meat dishes of all kinds, from simple steaks to hearty daubes.

Catena Malbec 2015
Mendoza 13% alc. $$-$$$

Catena is a well-known name in Argentine wine. This malbec is an excellent example of the variety, with rich, complex fruit that covers a wide spectrum of flavours, and a spine of fresh, well-tailored acidity. The tannins are easy going. If malbec seems made for beef, it's because they're paired so often in Argentina, which has the second-highest per capita consumption in the world. So drink it with steak, roast beef, and beef empanadas.

Clos de los Siete 2014
Valle de Uco, Mendoza 14.5% alc. $$$

The name refers to the estate of seven vineyards in the foothills of the Andes that is managed by well-known French winemaker Michel Rolland. The wine is a blend that's about half malbec with contributions from merlot, syrah, cabernet franc, and petit verdot. Year after year it's impressive, with well-defined and focused flavours, plenty of complexity, and excellent balance and harmony. It's quite full bodied and needs substantial food to accompany it. Roast beef and lamb are terrific candidates.

Fuzion 'Orgánico' Malbec-Cabernet 2017
Mendoza, Argentina 13% alc. $$

Made from organically farmed grapes, this blend of malbec and cabernet sauvignon is definitely fruit-driven but is equally definitely not a simple fruit-bomb. The flavours are concentrated and quite plush, but they're layered and also well supported by clean acidity. The wine has good structure and integrated tannins, and it's an easy match for burgers and barbecued ribs.

Kaiken 'Reserva Especial' Malbec 2016
Mendoza 13.5% $$

This is another very good quality malbec from Mendoza, the sprawling region that produces the bulk of Argentina's wine. Look for flavours that are well defined and focused. They're backed by fresh, clean acidity that's well balanced for the fruit. The tannins are negligible. This is a fairly fruity wine that's versatile at the table, It goes well with beef of course (it is from Argentina!) and with other red meats, but will extend to pork, burgers, and spicy sausages.

Kaiken 'Ultra' Leyenda Cabernet Sauvignon 2016
Mendoza 14% $$$

Cabernet Sauvignon from Argentina is often overshadowed by the better-known malbec from the country, but Argentina produces some spectacular examples. This one shows polished flavours with depth and breadth, all well complemented and balanced by a seam of fresh acidity. The tannins are drying and ripe, and very approachable. Overall it's dry and harmonious and a great choice for many red meat dishes.

ARGENTINA

Santa Julia is one of the brands of wine made by the Zuccardi family, one of Argentina's biggest producers. The family owned vineyards from the 1950s, but José Alberto Zuccardi kickstarted the modern winery in the 1990s and it is now responsible not only for the Santa Julia line but also for Fuzion, the brand that led the Argentine malbec invasion of the early 2000s. In addition to these popular brands, the Zuccardi family makes a number of high-quality wines, including those in the Zuccardi Q (for Quality) series.

La Linda 'Private Selection' Old Vines Malbec 2015
Mendoza 13.5% alc. $$

'Old Vines' is an unregulated term and what's 'old' in one region might be quite young in another. But by labelling a wine this way the producer is signalling that the wine has the particular intensity that often accompanies aging. This is certainly a wine with lots of complex fruit. Equally important, it's balanced and well-structured, with good acidity. That sets it up for the beef that Argentina is known for.

Luigi Bosca Malbec 2015
Mendoza 13.7% alc. $$-$$$

This is a dry red wine you can cellar through to the early-mid 2020s. Look for dense and layered fruit flavours that give the wine some robustness, but they're paired with the clean acidity to lighten the weight and make it very drinkable. It's had a year's aging in French barrels and the tannins are now well integrated. This is a natural for grilled steak and other similarly robust dishes.

Norton 'Barrel Select' Malbec 2017
Mendoza 13.5% alc $$

As the name suggests, this wine comes from selected American and French barrels that Norton uses to age their malbecs about 12 months. This is a delicious malbec that's driven by the fruit, which in turn is plush, flavour-filled, and persistent right through the palate. The acidity is fresh and clean, and the texture is soft. Beef is always the first thought when it comes to malbec because Argentina has the second highest per capita beef consumption in the world.

Norton Privada 2014
Mendoza 14% alc.   **$$$**

This is a robust and approachable blend of malbec (40%) and merlot and cabernet sauvignon (30%) each. The flavours are deep and broad with ripe sweetness at the core, and although it's a weighty wine it's quite light on its feet and very drinkable. The fruit-acid balance is very good, and all the components are well integrated. Drink it as Argentines would with beef.

Pascual Toso Malbec 2016
Mendoza 13.5% alc.   **$$**

Many of the pioneers of winemaking in Argentina were immigrants from Italy, such as Pascual Toso, who came from Piedmont and opened his winery in 1890. The rest is history, but the wine is current. This wine is a model of affordable malbec. It has solid and persistent flavours backed by clean, fresh acidity, with easy-going tannins. It's dry and medium bodied, and it goes well with beef and other red meats.

Pascual Toso 'Limited Edition' Malbec 2015
Mendoza 14% alc.   **$$**

There was a time that the world seemed awash with Mendoza malbec, and at that time Pascual Toso was a brand that stood out from the crowd. It still does, even though the flood of malbec has subsided. Here you'll find very attractive flavours that are well defined and very complex. The balance is excellent and the tannins are soft. It's an excellent choice for red meats in general, as well as for other Argentine treats such as empanadas.

Piattelli Reserve Cabernet Sauvignon 2016
Salta 14.5% alc. $$

The Salta wine region lies in the extreme north of Argentina, where the vineyards are situated at high elevations in the foothills of the Andes mountains. The intense sunshine and cool evenings make for excellent growing conditions for grapes that produce wines, like this one, that show gorgeous ripe fruit flavour and fresh acidity. This is an attractive and complex wine built for food. Beef is an obvious choice, but lamb, game meats, and rich pastas are also in this wine's orbit.

Santa Julia Reserva Cabernet Sauvignon 2016
Valle de Uco, Mendoza, Argentina 13% alc. $$

Argentine cabernet sauvignon is so much in the shadow of malbec that is often undervalued and under-appreciated. But Argentina makes many fine cabernets and even the entry-level examples, like this one from the Zuccardi family, are very good quality and value. You'll find good complexity in the concentrated flavours, good fruit-acid balance, and light tannins. It's wine for red meats and it will extend to richer pork and poultry dishes, too.

Santa Julia Reserva Malbec 2016
Valle de Uco, Mendoza, Argentina 13.5% alc. $$

This is a quite lovely malbec, not least because it's a change from the full-bodied style that malbec often comes in. This one is light-to-medium in weight, with attractive fruit flavours and good acidity to keep it fresh and food-versatile. Drink this with chicken, turkey, and pork, as well as with pastas and lightly spiced empanadas.

Santa Julia 'Magna' Malbec-Cabernet 2016
Valle de Uco, Mendoza, Argentina 13% alc. $$

This blend combines malbec, which is Argentina's signature red grape variety, with cabernet sauvignon, a variety that can produce stunning wines in that country. Here you get a well-priced red with concentrated flavours that are solid right through the palate, backed by clean acidity, with drying, well-integrated tannins. It's a well-balanced wine you can enjoy with myriad grilled meats, especially beef and lamb, as well as with well-seasoned sausages.

Tilia Malbec 2017
Mendoza 12.5% alc. $$

This is a slightly lighter style of malbec than many, but it still conveys the concentrated fruit flavours that you expect of the variety. Here they persist right through the palate and show decent complexity, and they're complemented by fresh, balanced acidity. With negligible tannins, this goes well with red meats, and it will also extend to many pork and richer poultry dishes, especially if they're prepared in red wine.

Trapiche 'Broquel' Malbec 2016
Mendoza 14% alc. $$

Look for quite robust flavours in this full-flavoured malbec. There's quite decent complexity and some depth to the fruit, which is supported by a good level of acidity. The tannins are moderately gripping. It's dry and medium bodied and it goes well with beef (like all malbecs), other red and game meats, and with hearty meat dishes of many kinds.

Trapiche Reserve Cabernet Sauvignon 2016
Mendoza 13.5% alc. $$

Trapiche produces a wide range of quality wines and is to the fore in exploring new wine regions in Argentina. This cabernet is from Mendoza, by far the country's largest and best-known region, and it's a credit to the winery. Look for lovely, well-defined fruit flavours right through the palate and a supporting seam of fresh and clean acidity. The tannins are relaxed. This is a great choice for red meats, burgers, and many things off the grill.

Trapiche Reserve Malbec 2016
Mendoza 13.5% alc. $$

It's not surprising to see so many malbecs in any line-up of red wines from Argentina because the variety dominates the country's vineyards—it occupies more than twice the area of the next common red variety, bonarda. This example, from Trapiche, is well made and versatile. You'll find it fruit-driven and well structured, with concentrated and reasonably complex flavours, and very good balance. Drink it with burgers, grilled sausages, ribs, and braised red meats.

Trapiche Reserve Merlot 2016
Mendoza 14% alc. $$

You don't really think merlot when you think of Argentina, but this is more evidence that the country is more than malbec. This is a quite lovely merlot with some plushness and fleshiness to the flavours and texture and very good balance in the fruit-acidity relationship. It has relaxed and integrated tannins and it pairs well with red meats and hearty dishes that feature poultry and pork.

AUSTRALIA

19 Crimes Cabernet Sauvignon 2016
Limestone Coast 14% alc.   **$$–$$$**

Limestone Coast is a South Australia wine region well known for producing fine cabernet sauvignons. This is a very good and affordable example—despite the rather grim label showing the mug shot of a convict destined for the penal colonies of Australia. (There were no penal colonies in South Australia.) The wine itself is full of ripe, concentrated, and well-layered fruit that's effectively backed by fresh acidity. Dry and full-bodied, it's a natural for red meats.

19 Crimes Shiraz-Durif 2016
Victoria 14.5% alc.   **$$–$$$**

Named for the 19 crimes in English law for which criminals could be transported to Australia (although none to Victoria) from the late 1700s, this is a robust blend that shows quite intense flavours. At the same time, the fruit is well structured and the acidity complements it well. It would be a crime not to pair this with hearty red meat dishes. On the other hand, if you were transported to Australia, you'd find a terrific range of wines to greet you there.

Angove Organic Cabernet Sauvignon 2016
South Australia 14.5% alc.   **$$**

The alcohol is fairly high in this cabernet sauvignon, perhaps a reflection of warming growing conditions. As far as tasting the wine is concerned, the good news is that the alcohol is imperceptible on the nose and palate. In fact all the components are balanced: the concentrated and well-layered fruit, the clean and calibrated acid, and the light tannins. This is an excellent wine for red meat and hearty stews.

Angove Organic Shiraz 2017
South Australia 14% alc. $$

The label shouts ORGANIC in bold black on white, so if you're looking for a wine made from organically grown grapes you won't have trouble spotting this one. It's a fruit-driven shiraz in the familiar Australian style, with quite intense flavours right through the palate. The structure, balance, and acidity are good, and it's a natural for barbecued ribs with that sticky sauce.

Angove Grenache-Shiraz-Mourvèdre 2016
McLaren Vale 14% alc. $$$

Often abbreviated GSM, this is a fairly common blend of three varieties whose styles vary from place to place. Here you have an excellent Australian example from one of the country's prestigious regions: McLaren Vale in South Australia. The flavours are concentrated and complex, with a core of ripe-sweet fruit, the acid is balanced, and the tannins are relaxed. This is a natural for red meats, especially grilled beef and lamb and well-seasoned sausages.

Angove Shiraz 2016
McLaren Vale 14.5% alc. $$

The tide of Australian shiraz that washed over the world a couple of decades ago has receded to some extent, but some real beauties remain in Canadian markets. This is one, a richly flavoured and textured shiraz that leads with fruit and achieves excellent balance. The acidity is clean and fresh and the tannins are well integrated. You can't go wrong pouring this with red meats, especially grilled lamb.

Banrock Station Shiraz 2015
South Eastern Australia 13% alc. $$

Banrock Station is noted for its commitment to

supporting environmental causes, especially wetland, waterway, and wildlife conservation in many parts of the world. So you can feel good as you sip this shiraz. It's fruit-driven, with ripe-sweet flavours that are nicely layered and backed by clean acidity. Enjoy it with burgers, grilled sausages, and red meats.

Barossa Valley Estate Shiraz 2016
Barossa Valley 14% alc. $$$

Fruit-driven, with concentrated flavours of ripe-sweet fruit, this is made in a classic Australian style of shiraz—in the best sense. It's not over-the-top, like some wines that just overpower your palate and any nearby food. Instead, it's well defined and structured, with well-balanced acidity that keeps the fruit honest. The tannins are well integrated and you can enjoy this with many red meats.

Grant Burge 'The Holy Trinity' Grenache-Shiraz-Mourvèdre 2013
Barossa Valley, Australia 14% alc. $$$-$$$$

These three grape varieties have indeed become a sort of Holy Trinity, as the blend (often referred to as GSM) is made in many parts of the wine-producing world. In this case the style is focused on plush, forward fruit that's quite intensely flavoured and well layered. It's supported by fresh acidity and shows tannins that are easy-going. This is a big, well-structured wine that calls for big food, such as grilled lamb and steak.

Hope's End Red Blend 2016
South Australia 13.5% alc. $$

Hope must surely have ended not only for convicts transported to Australia in the 1800s but also for many settlers who arrived from the other side of the world. Quite why this scenario inspired this wine isn't clear, but no matter. It's full of sweet-ripe fruit backed by just enough fresh acidity. It has a round, soft text and no tannins to speak of, and it goes well with burgers, barbecued ribs, and grilled sausages.

Kilikanoon 'Killerman's Run' Shiraz 2014
Clare Valley, Australia 14.5% alc $$

This is a robust, full-bodied, yet remarkably easy-drinking shiraz that the producer suggests cooling down a little more than usual for red wine. It's good adviceand not only for this red wine. Look for rich, concentrated flavours with plenty of complexity, and well-balanced acidity. The alcohol is relatively high, but it's unobtrusive in the aromas and flavours. Enjoy this shiraz with red meats, especially grilled lamb.

Lindeman's 'Bin 50' Shiraz 2017
South Eastern Australia 13.5% alc. $$

Dr. Lindeman, who founded this winery, advocated temperance in drinking but at the same time believed that wine had important medicinal qualities. Drinking wine, then, was a matter of health as of pleasure. This shiraz, described on the label as 'smooth and suave' is led by the fruit, which is concentrated and decidedly up-front. The acid is clean and fresh, and the tannins are relaxed. It's an easy choice for burgers, kebabs, and ribs.

Lindeman's 'Gentleman's Collection' Cabernet Sauvignon 2016
South Eastern Australia 14% alc. $$

The story goes that Dr. Lindeman, who founded this winery, encouraged the hard-working, hard-drinking men around him to be more gentlemanly—more like him. We can wonder if it involved drinking wine from a glass rather than from the bottle, as I recommend for this cabernet sauvignon. It'll help you appreciate the concentrated flavours and very good fruit-acid balance. I suggest pairing it with grilled red meats—eaten with a knife and fork, as a gentleman would.

Penfolds 'Koonunga Hill' Shiraz Cabernet 2016
South Australia 14.5% alc. $$-$$$

Although the shiraz-cabernet sauvignon blend is made elsewhere, Australia has made it its own, and the first Penfolds blend carrying this name was made in 1976, more than 40 years ago. Look for rich, ripe fruit in this example. There are layers of complexity with a tangy, fresh texture from the well-calibrated acid. It's dry with moderate tannins and is a great bed for red meats.

Penfolds 'Thomas Hyland' Shiraz 2016
South Ausralia 14.5% alc. $$-$$$

This is an almost-full-bodied, luscious shiraz named for the founder's son-in-law. It has assertive flavours with very god complexity and breadth, and a texture that's plush and dense. The acidity is clean and fresh, and very well balanced with the fruit, and the tannins are quite relaxed. This is a real pleasure to drink with many foods, but it goes especially well with roast or grilled lamb.

Red Knot Cabernet Sauvignon 2016
McLaren Vale 14% alc. $$

There's an image of tangled thread on the label and it's sort of echoed in the plastic capsule. It's not exactly a knot, but you need to unravel it to get to the wine, so it's effectively a knot. But the wine inside is the important thing, and it's definitely worth trying. This is a fruit-driven cabernet with quite rich flavours. It's quite complex, well

AUSTRALIA
Penfolds is one of Australia's oldest wineries, having been founded in 1844—which means they celebrate their 175th anniversary in 2019. The founder was Dr. Thomas Penfold, who began to make wine to give to his patients for medical purposes. That reason has long gone by the board, and Penfolds is now about prescribing pleasure. They're most famous for Grange, a top-of-the-line, almost-100% shiraz that sells for hundreds of dollars a bottle on release. But equally remarkable is the attention the Penfolds winemaking team, led by chief winemaker Peter Gago, gives to making fine wines at much more affordable prices.

balanced, and it goes very well with burgers, red meats, and many foods from the barbecue.

Red Knot Shiraz 2016
McLaren Vale 14% alc. $$

The McLaren Vale wine region, to the south of Adelaide in South Australia, has a reputation for making fine wines. This shiraz delivers lovely fruit that rises above the merely rich fruit of many shirazes at this price. The flavours are ripe and layered, with good structure, and the balanced acidity adds freshness to the texture. The tannins are negligible. This is a very easy wine to pair with red meats, burgers, and grilled sausages.

Rosemount Estate 'Diamond Label' Shiraz 2017
South Australia 13.5% alc. $$

Rosemount Estate shiraz has been a Canadian staple for many years. It's not the most complicated wine in the world, but it delivers a style of shiraz that's very popular: solid, ripe fruit flavours, good fruit-acid balance, and the easiest of easy-going tannins. This is a terrific choice when you're barbecuing burgers, ribs, and steaks.

Rymill 'The Yearling' Cabernet Sauvignon 2015
Coonawarra 14.5% alc. $$

The Coonawarra wine region of South Australia is known for cabernet sauvignon and you'll find that this is a very good example of what it produces at an affordable price. Look for concentrated flavour with good complexity and some breadth, well-balanced fresh acidity, and a light tannic grip that's easily managed. It's medium-weight and goes well with pork, red meats, and burgers.

The Thief Grenache-Shiraz-Mataro 2015
Barossa Valley 14% alc. $$$

There's a story about the winemaker's great-great-grandfather and a cow on the back label, together with a wry suggestion that the wine is 'best enjoyed with beef dishes.' This GSM blend (see the grape varieties in the name of the wine) is full of rich flavours that are complex and well structured. The acidity is well balanced and the tannins are moderate. It's a big and slightly rustic wine, and very enjoyable. And yes, enjoy it with beef.

Thorn-Clarke Barossa Grenache-Shiraz 2016
Barossa Valley 14.5% alc. $$

Thorn-Clarke makes a wide range of wines from its vineyards in the Barossa Valley, which is home to some of Australia's best shiraz vineyards. This blend, which includes the increasingly popular grenache variety, delivers very good complexity in the concentrated and well-defined flavours. The acidity is perfectly calibrated, and the tannins are relaxed. This goes easily with red meats, but it also extends to many pork and poultry dishes.

Thorn-Clarke 'Shotfire' Quartage 2015
Barossa Valley 14.5% alc. $$$

This is a really compelling blend of cabernet sauvignon, cabernet franc, petit verdot, and merlot—four of the red varieties permitted in Bordeaux. Look for lovely rich and well-structured flavours here, along with well-balanced, fresh and clean acidity. The tannins are moderately gripping, but easily managed. The overall balance and harmony are very good, and this is an excellent pairing with roast beef or lamb.

Thorn-Clarke 'Shotfire' Shiraz 2016
Barossa Valley 14.5% alc. $$$

When contemplating the vast array of Australian shirazes on the market, it's worth remembering that not all were created equal. Some come from superior growing areas, some were made by superior hands. This definitely sits high in the superior ranks. The fruit is focused and well defined, the acidity is right-on, and the overall balance is impressive. Drink it with red meats, of course, and don't hesitate to open it on a special occasion.

Thorn-Clarke 'Terra Barossa' Shiraz 2017
Barossa Valley 14.5% alc. $$

This is a really lovely wine that delivers all you want from a well-made Barossa shiraz, and adds a bit more. The fruit is impressive, through and through, with focused and quite nuanced flavours. The spine of acidity is perfectly calibrated to the fruit, resulting in impressive balance, and the tannins are ripe, drying, and eminently manageable. This shiraz is built for red meat, so why disappoint it? Game, lamb, and beef are all candidates.

Vasse Felix 'Filius' Cabernet Sauvignon 2015
Margaret River, Australia 14% alc $$$-$$$$

This is a very impressive cabernet sauvignon from a region that's become known for its cabernets. It's what I think of as a complete wine, with finely layered and focused flavours supported by a spine of fresh, clean acidity. The tannins are soft and integrated and all the components are in harmony. Enjoy this with a rack of lamb or a rib-eye steak.

Wakefield Cabernet Sauvignon 2016
Clare Valley 14% alc. $$

The Clare Valley wine region, close to Adelaide in

South Australia, is well known for its red wines and this cabernet sauvignon delivers superior quality across the board. Look for well-measured fruit flavours that are well layered and structured. The fruit-acid balance is excellent, and the tannins are lightly gripping. It's dry and medium-bodied, and it goes really well with many red meats.

Wolf Blass 'Red Label' Cabernet-Merlot 2016
South-Eastern Australia 13.5% alc. $$

The South Eastern Australia wine zone is a vast area that includes most of Australia's wine production. Labelling a bottle this way means that producers can source grapes from anywhere in the zone. This cabernet sauvignon-merlot blend shows concentrated, well-layered, ripe fruit supported by clean, fresh acidity. The tannins are negligible. It's a straightforward red that goes well with red meats, burgers, and ribs.

Wolf Blass 'Yellow Label' Cabernet Sauvignon 2016
McLaren Vale, Langhorne Creek 13.5% alc. $$

This is a well-made cabernet sauvignon that has very good varietal character. Look for complexity in the well-defined flavours, and for a seam of fresh, clean acidity that supports and animates the fruit. Tannins are light and nicely integrated. Overall, it's an attractive and very drinkable cabernet, and it goes very well with red meats, hearty pastas and stews, as well as with many foods from the barbecue.

Wolf Blass 'Yellow Label' Pinot Noir 2016
Adelaide Hills, Yarra Valley 13.5% alc. $$

Sourced from vineyards in two regions in different states, this is a well-made and very satisfying pinot noir. It delivers very attractive flavours that lie between understated and positive and that are complex and focused. The acidity is clean and balanced and the tannins are relaxed. This is a very good choice for many poultry and pork dishes, for grilled salmon, and for medium-strength cheeses.

Wolf Blass 'Yellow Label' Shiraz 2016
Langhorne Creek, McLaren Vale 13.5% alc. $$

For many years, much Australian shiraz was jammy with over-ripe fruit, low in alcohol, and lacking much complexity, and they overpowered any food that came near. Distinctive shirazes could be hard to come by. But this example, from two premium South Australian regions, delivers nicely focused flavours, good layering and structure, and very good balance. It's a fine food wine that goes well with many red meat dishes.

Yalumba 'The Strapper' Grenache-Shiraz-Mataro 2015
Barossa Valley 13.5% alc. $$

The GSM blend (the first letter of each variety) works whether the S stands for syrah or shiraz (two names for the same variety) or the M for mataro or mourvèdre (ditto). This Yalumba example delivers great quality from start to finish. The flavours are robust and structured and the supporting acidity is refreshing and clean. The tannins are low-to-moderate and easily manageable. This is great with well-seasoned red meat dishes, such as braised lamb shanks and steak with a peppercorn sauce.

Yalumba 'The Y Series' Shiraz 2017
South Australia 13.5% alc. $$

Yalumba's 'Y Series' offers red and white wines of high quality and affordable prices and this shiraz fits that profile admirably. The flavour profile is packed with fruit that's defined and structured, while the supporting acidity is clean, fresh, and tailored to the weight of the fruit. It's a dry, medium-plus bodied wine, and a great candidate if you're eating fairly robust red meat dishes.

Yellow Tail Shiraz 2016
South Eastern Australia 13.5% alc. $$

This was extraordinarily popular when it was first released, and it still has a strong following. It's a fruity wine with jammy flavours with some sweet-ripeness. They're supported by good acidity that tends to be a little on the low side, making this a slightly 'fat' wine. You'll find this is a very good wine for barbecued ribs, burgers, and grilled sausages, and that it also goes well with meat-lovers' pizzas.

CANADA—BRITISH COLUMBIA
Clos du Soleil Célestiale 2014
BC VQA British Columbia 14.2% alc. $$$

This is a terrific red blend that brings together merlot (38%), cabernet sauvignon (36%), cabernet franc (20%), malbec (5%), and petit verdot (1%). It's Clos du Soleil's signature wine and it delivers across the board. The flavours are concentrated and complex, the acidity is perfectly calibrated to the fruit, and the tannins are dry and approachable. Overall it's an excellent wine and it goes well with many red meat dishes as well as hearty pastas and risottos.

Clos du Soleil Signature 2014
BC VQA Similkameen Valley 14.8% alc. $$$$$

This is a really lovely blend of cabernet sauvignon, merlot, petit verdot, cabernet franc, and malbec—five of the red varieties permitted in Bordeaux. The flavours are quite gorgeous, with both depth and breadth, and with complexity and structure. The acidity is well tailored to the fruit, and the tannins are ripe with a light grip. This is a terrific wine for a rack of lamb or a juicy sirloin steak.

Five Vineyards Cabernet-Merlot 2015
BC VQA Okanagan Valley 14% alc. $$

This is a straightforward, uncomplicated, but very drinkable red blend, named for the Okanagan Valley vineyards that Mission Hill can draw grapes from. You'll find the flavours consistent right through the palate and backed by balanced and fresh acidity. The tannins are relaxed and this is an easy choice if you're looking for a red to go with burgers, barbecued ribs, and all manner of red meats.

Five Vineyards Pinot Noir 2016
BC VQA Okanagan Valley 13% alc. $$

This is a very well-priced pinot noir for the quality of the wine. It's a mid-range pinot style that's medium-weight, has positive but not too concentrated fruit, and delivers a dose of fresh, food-friendly acidity. It's quite complex and all the components are very well balanced. This is a good choice for roast or grilled lamb, grilled duck breast, and for richer poultry dishes, such as coq au vin.

Mission Hill Reserve Cabernet Sauvignon 2015
BC VQA Okanagan Valley 14.5% alc. $$$$

This is a full bodied cabernet sauvignon that sits in the higher tiers of Mission Hill's offerings. Look for plenty of ripe fruit flavours that have depth as well as breadth, a lot of complexity, and some real finesse. The acidity is spot-on, and the tannins are firm and manageable. Overall it's an impressive and delicious wine that you can enjoy with roasted or grilled red meats and hearty daubes.

Monte Creek Ranch Reserve Pinot Noir 2016
BC VQA British Columbia 13% alc. $$$$

This very attractive pinot noir has quite substantial fruit, which means that it pairs well not only with the

CANADA—BRITISH COLUMBIA

Mission Hill Estate Wines is located in West Kelowna in the Okanagan Valley, and is the brainchild of Anthony von Mandl, who had been a wine merchant. Von Mandl purchased the abandoned Mission Hill winery in 1981 and at first bought grapes to make wine. In the 1990s he oversaw the rebuilding of the property in its present form as the region's pre-eminent destination winery. It has signal features, notably a 12-storey bell-tower, and includes a loggia, restaurant, and amphitheatre. Von Mandl also bought vineyards in the Okanagan Valley (they lie behind the name of the winery's Five Vineyards line) and they are the sole source of the Estate wines and the wines in the Legacy Collection, such as Oculus, an iconic Bordeaux blend.

lighter flavours of chicken and turkey, but will stand up well to more substantial red meat dishes—and many things in between. The wine has focused, well-defined flavours and they're supported by perfectly balanced clean, fresh acidity. It's dry with integrated tannins.

Quails' Gate Old Vines Reserve Foch 2015
BC VQA Okanagan Valley 14% alc.   **$$$**

This is made from the maréchal foch variety, a hybrid created in France that can make fine wines in the right hands. A pair of such hands clearly exists at Quails' Gate, because this is a lovely wine with focused and complex flavours supported by a broad seam of fresh acidity. It's medium bodied and the texture has the juiciness that invites food. You can drink this with many dishes, including poultry, pork, and red meats.

Quails' Gate Pinot Noir 2016
BC VQA Okanagan Valley 13.5% alc.   **$$$**

Sourced from 20-year-old vines, this is a lovely pinot noir. It's totally dry and fruit-driven, with concentrated and well-layered flavours complemented with fresh acidity. The texture is fairly plush and very smooth, with the tannins well integrated. It's a harmonious pinot noir that does well with mushroom risotto, coq au vin, and many other dishes.

Quails' Gate 'Stewart Family Reserve' Pinot Noir 2016
BC VQA Okanagan Valley 13.5% alc.   **$$$$$**

This really lovely pinot noir sits in the top tier of Quails' Gate wines that's named for the Stewart family that owns the winery. Look for focused and nuanced flavours right through the palate and a spine of edgy acidity. The tannins are well integrated and the wine is balanced in every respect. It's got the weight to handle red meats and the finesse that suits it to lighter white meats, poultry, and dark fish.

Road 13 5th Element Red 2013
BC VQA British Columbia 15.5% alc. $$$$

This is an impressive blend of merlot (45%), syrah (18%), cabernet sauvignon (19%), cabernet franc (13%), and petit verdot (5%)—impressive not because it's a wine that knocks you over with power, but because it impresses with finesse. The high alcohol level is imperceptible on the nose and palate, the flavours are nuanced and structured, and the fruit-acid balance is right-on. With integrated tannins, this is an excellent partner for roast beef and lamb.

Road 13 'Honest John's' Red 2016
BC VQA British Columbia 14.4% alc. $$-$$$

Most of the wine in this blend comes from merlot (43%), gamay noir (26%), and pinot noir (16%), with small percentages of syrah, viognier, and cabernet franc. It's a fairly big-boned, fruit-driven wine, with plenty of concentrated flavour. The core gives off ripe-sweet fruit, and the flavours are well supported by fresh acidity. The tannins are very relaxed. This is a great wine for well-seasoned barbecued meats of all kind, including burgers, steaks, and ribs.

CANADA–NOVA SCOTIA
Coastal Maréchal Foch-Marquette 2015
Nova Scotia 12% alc. $$

This blend of maréchal foch and the even less-known variety, marquette, was aged for six months in French barrels. It shows quite concentrated flavours (and a hint of smokiness) balanced by bright, clean acidity. The style is reminiscent of a lighter pinot noir, and you can pair it with the dishes that pinot often goes well with, such as poultry, pork, grilled salmon, and mushroom risotto.

CANADA—ONTARIO

Arterra Pinot Noir 2015
VQA Niagara Peninsula 13% alc. $$$$

This is a very elegant pinot noir that shows beautiful, well-defined and focused flavours in a profile that's both broad and deep. The acidity is spot-on, expertly calibrated to the fruit, and the tannins are present and manageable. It's impressive overall and it's above all very drinkable. It's a great choice for classic Burgundy dishes such as coq au vin, and it not only pairs well with many chicken and pork dishes but will easily extend to lamb.

Bachelder Wismer-Parke Vineyard Pinot Noir 2014
VQA Twenty Mile Bench 13% alc. $$$$

Thomas Bachelder is a winemaker and consultant, based in the Niagara Peninsula region, who focuses on chardonnay and pinot noir. This single-vineyard pinot noir is a real standout. It more than delivers on fruit quality and complexity and on fruit-acid balance and it's an elegant wine you can drink now or hold to the early 2020s. It's dry and medium-bodied, and you can enjoy it with coq au vin, grilled lamb, and duck breast.

Cave Spring Gamay 2016
VQA Niagara Escarpment 13% alc. $$-$$$

Gamay, the variety found in the wines of Beaujolais, grows well and makes excellent wines in Ontario—to the point that some people believe it should be Ontario's signature red grape variety. Cave Spring's gamay is full of bright, well-layered fruit, perfectly matched to clean, vibrant acidity. It's very versatile at the table, where you can partner it with poultry, pork, and salmon.

Cave Spring Pinot Noir 2016
Niagara Escarpment 12.5% alc. $$

This is a fairly robust pinot noir for Niagara, but it doesn't lose sight of its inner pinot-ness. Look for concentrated and well-layered fruit harnessed to a very well-tailored level of acidity that's clean and positive. It's dry and medium-bodied, with the ripe tannins well integrated. This is an easy match for poultry and pork, and it will also take on red meat dishes, too.

Cave Spring Cabernet Franc 2016
VQA Niagara Peninsula 13.5% alc. $$-$$$

Cabernet franc is Ontario's most-planted quality red grape variety, and it's just coming into its own in a growing number of 100% varietal wines (rather than being a component in Bordeaux blends). This example from Cave Spring shows quite plush and concentrated flavours with good complexity, all backed by fresh acidity. There's a slight, attractive herbaceous note that's quite typical. Drink this with red meats, burgers, and meat pies.

Château des Charmes Cabernet-Merlot 2016
VQA Niagara-on-the-Lake 13% alc. $$

Cabernets sauvignon and franc work well with merlot, each bringing its qualities to the blend. It's a classic case, in the world of wine, of the sum being greater than the parts. This example, from one of Niagara's most reliable bigger wineries, delivers attractive flavours across the palate, with good complexity and structure. It's dry and medium-bodied, with very good fruit-acid balance and easy-going tannins. Drink it with white meats and lighter red meat dishes.

Château des Charmes Equuleus 2014
VQA St. David's Bench 13.6% alc. $$$$

Equuleus is the signature red wine of Château des Charmes and it recognizes both the Little Horse constellation that appears in the sky at harvest time and the passion of Paul Bosc Sr., founder of the winery, for Egyptian Arabian horses. This is an elegant blend of cabernet sauvignon (50%), cabernet franc, and merlot (25% each). The fruit profile is broad and deep and the fruit-acid balance is right-on. Enjoy it with grilled and roasted red meats.

Château des Charmes Gamay Noir 2016
VQA Niagara-on-the-Lake 13% alc. $$

Gamay is the grape of Beaujolais, although very few wines from that region are labelled by the variety. It grows very successfully in Ontario and this is a really attractive example. The fruit flavours are bright and serious, with good concentration and complexity. The acidity is very refreshing and the tannins are negligible (as is usual with gamay). It's very versatile with food. Drink it with grilled salmon, chicken, pork, and with moderately strong cheeses.

EastDell Gamay Noir 2016
VQA Niagara Peninsula 13% alc. $$

Gamay, the grape variety made famous by Beaujolais, grows very successfully in Ontario, and Ontario producers make it in a number of styles. This one is fairly robust, with full-on fruit that's complex and dense, supported by clean, fresh acidity. It's a well-made gamay that you can pair with weightier red meat dishes, as well as poultry, pork, and hearty vegetarian risotttos.

MENDOZA REGION, ARGENTINA

Fielding Cabernet Franc 2016
VQA Niagara Peninsula 13.4% alc. $$$

Cabernet franc is a bit of a sleeper variety—known to many people as a component is many red blends, but just coming into its own as a single-variety wine in many regions around the world. This is a very attractive example from Fielding's winemaker, Richie Roberts. It shows lovely, well-layered and focused fruit, fresh and clean acidity, and moderate tannins. It's a fresh, serious, and easy-drinking wine. Drink it with red meats such as braised lamb shank and juicy steak.

Fielding Red Conception 2016
VQA Niagara Peninsula 13% alc. $$-$$$

It seems that one of Fielding's vineyards was once a popular 'parking' place for young people, and that more than grapes might have been produced there. Hence the name of this wine. It's a very attractive blend of merlot, cabernet sauvignon, cabernet franc, and syrah. The flavours are concentrated and focused and there's very good fruit-acid balance. Dry and medium bodied, it's a red you can enjoy with red and white meats.

Flat Rock Cellars Pinot Noir 2016
VQA Twenty Mile Bench 13.5% alc. $$$

Flat Rock Cellars is named for the flat rocks that were discovered when the land was being excavated to create the winery. This is a medium-bodied pinot noir from the warm 2016 Ontario vintage. It's characterized by quite concentrated and complex red fruit flavours that are well supported by the acidity you look for in pinot noir. The tannins are ripe and easy-going, and this is an excellent partner for roast turkey and chicken, as well as for pork dishes.

Henry of Pelham 'House Wine' Baco-Cabernet Sauvignon 2016
VQA Ontario 13.5% alc. $$

This blend of baco noir and cabernet sauvignon delivers some funkiness and smokiness thanks to the baco. Otherwise it's an ever-so-slightly sweet, straightforward red that makes a very good wine for parties or for casual meals of hamburgers or grilled seasoned sausages. It's mid-weight, with fairly concentrated flavours and good acidity that cleans up the light sweetness on the finish.

Henry of Pelham 'Sibling Rivalry' Red 2016
VQA Niagara Peninsula 13% alc. $$

This is a blend of merlot, cabernet franc, and cabernet sauvignon. It's essentially dry, with quite rich flavours that are decently layered and balanced by fresh acidity. It's not a complicated wine, but it's easy-drinking and is versatile with food. Drink it with all sorts of meat—poultry, beef, pork —as well as with hearty tomato-based pasta dishes.

Henry of Pelham Pinot Noir 2016
VQA Niagara Peninsula 13% alc. $$

The cool-climate growing conditions of Niagara Peninsula can make for some very attractive pinot noirs in a fairly lean style. This example shows fruit that is high-toned and consistent right through the palate and supported by a spine of bright, clean acidity. It's a well-balanced, dry wine with easy-going tannins, and it goes well with mushroom risotto, grilled salmon, and many poultry dishes.

Henry of Pelham Cabernet-Merlot 2016
VQA Niagara Peninsula 13.5% alc. $$

This is an attractive cab-merlot blend that brings together concentrated fruit flavours that are decently complex and defined with fresh, clean acidity and easygoing tannins. The fruit-acid balance is excellent and there's some juiciness to the texture, a quality that always seems to be an invitation to eat. This is a medium-bodied wine that's very versatile with food. You can pair it with chicken (say, coq-au-vin), pork, and red meats, as well as with stronger cheeses.

Henry of Pelham Baco Noir 2017
VQA Ontario 13% alc. $$

Henry of Pelham really brought baco noir to public attention by treating it as a serious grape with the potential to make quality wines. This is a nice example, delivering flavours that are concentrated, somewhat grapey, and decently complex. The acidity is well measured for the fruit, and the tannins are relaxed. It's more mainstream than the funky wine that baco can make and it goes well with barbecued ribs, chicken, and red meats.

Henry of Pelham Pinot Noir 2016
VQA Niagara Peninsula 13% alc. $$

Pinot noir is one of the strengths of the Niagara Peninsula region, and this one from Henry of Pelham is a very attractive example. The flavours are concentrated, well defined, and persistent from start to finish. They're supported by well-calibrated, clean acidity, while the tannins are ripe and integrated. Dry and medium-bodied, this is a great choice for lamb and duck, as well as for grilled Atlantic salmon.

Sue Ann Staff 'Bank Barn' Baco Noir 2016
VQA Ontario 10.4% alc. $$

Baco noir is a hybrid variety that's widely planted in Ontario. Often scorned because it's a hybrid and not a

CANADA—ONTARIO

Henry of Pelham is run by the three Speck brothers: Daniel, Matthew, and Paul. They helped their father plant the original estate vineyard on ancestral property in the late 1980s and they carried on the project after his sudden death before the winery opened. Now one of Niagara's most reliable wine-producers, Henry of Pelham makes a wide range of quality wines but has earned a reputation above all for red and sparkling wines. Cuvée Catharine white and rosé sparkling wines and Carte Blanche blanc de blancs are well-known as high quality bubblies. Henry of Pelham also pioneered the making of quality wines from the baco noir variety.

'noble' vitis vinifera variety, it has been rehabilitated by several producers who have made quality wine from it. It comes in varying styles, and this one veers toward the funky style that delivers grapey and smoky flavours. With good acidity and relaxed tannins, it's very attractive and a good pairing for barbecued ribs.

Sue-Anne Staff 'Fancy Farm Girl' Red 2013
VQA Niagara Peninsula 12.5% alc. $$

This is quite a delicious red blend. There just a touch of sweetness, which many people will enjoy, and the flavours are fruity, concentrated, and bright. The acidity clicks in well to keep the flavours in line (and to mute the light sweetness) and there are some drying tannins for added complexity. This goes very well with sauce-basted ribs and chicken.

Tawse 'Quarry Road Vineyard' Pinot Noir 2015
VQA Vinemount Ridge 12.5% alc. $$$

Tawse's Director of Winemaking Paul Pender does a great job with pinot noir, and this single-vineyard example is an excellent example. It's on the lighter side of the pinot noir spectrum, but it delivers solid and focused fruit right through the palate. The acidity is fresh and clean, adding some juiciness to the wine, and the tannins are easy-going. Drink it with chicken, turkey, duck, grilled salmon, and with medium-strength cheeses.

Thirteenth Street Burger Blend 2016
VQA Niagara Peninsula 13% alc. $$

No need to guess what the winery thinks you ought to pair this with. It's a blend of gamay and pinot noir, both key red varieties in Burgundy, and both similar in many respects. Blending them amplifies the similarities to give you solid, persistent, high-toned fruit, juicy acidity, and light tannic grip. Overall it makes on a wine that's very friendly to food and I'd go well beyond burgers to include pork, poultry, and red meats in general.

Wayne Gretsky 'No. 99' Cabernet-Merlot 2016
VQA Niagara Peninsula 12.5% alc. $$

Gretzky scores easily with this cabernet-merlot blend. It delivers concentrated and nicely defined flavours through the palate and they're supported by well-balanced, fresh acidity. It's a refreshing mouthful with negligible tannins and the measured fruit and good acidity make it easy to pair with food. You could drink this with red meats, but it has the versatility to pair well with chicken and pork.

CHILE

Caliterra Reserva Cabernet Sauvignon 2016
DO Valle de Colchagua 13.5% alc. $$

This is a straightforward, uncomplicated cabernet sauvignon. It won't make you gasp with pleasure, but it's a well-made wine that succeeds at what it was intended to do: be an affordable red you can serve on diverse occasions. The fruit is concentrated, the acid is balanced, and the tannins are integrated. You can serve it with red meats, burgers, seasoned sausages, and many other foods from the barbecue.

Carmen Gran Reserva Cabernet Sauvignon 2015
DO Valle del Maipo 14% alc. $$

The Maipo Valley is Chile's most noted region for cabernet sauvignon. Little wonder, if it produces cabernets of this quality. It's definitely in a New World style that's fruit-driven and full of concentrated flavour. But it's no fruit-bomb. It delivers excellent structure and balance, and you'll find plenty of complexity here. It's ready to drink, but you could hold it to the mid-2020s. But why wait? It goes very well with red meats, especially grilled.

Carmen 'Premier' Reserva Carmenère 2015
Chile 13% alc. $$

When carmenère was discovered growing in Chile in 1994 (see the longer story below) it was in the vineyards of the Carmen winery. Even though the similarity in name is entirely coincidental, you'd expect Carmen to go out of their way to make an excellent carmenère, and they haven't disappointed. Look for lovely, focused flavours, excellent balance, and a full, juicy texture. It's an obvious choice for red meats.

Casillero del Diablo Cabernet Sauvignon 2016
DO Valle Central, Chile 13.5% alc. $$

This is a nicely made and affordable cabernet sauvignon that goes well with red meats, hearty stews and meat-based pasta, and many foods from the barbecue. Look for well-measured fruit with good concentration and layering, supported by fresh acidity. It's dry, medium-bodied, and lightly tannic. Overall, it's a straightforward, uncomplicated, and well-balanced red that is very versatile.

Casillero del Diablo Carmenère 2016
DO Valle Central, Chile 13.5% alc. $$

Carmenère originated in Bordeaux and was thought to have become extinct in the late 1800s. But some had been planted in Chile decades earlier, and it was discovered growing there in 1994—although it had been thought to be a clone of merlot. Since then, many Chilean producers have embraced it. This example has delicious flavours, good complexity, bright and clean acidity, and easy-going tannins. It's very enjoyable with richer red meat and game dishes.

Casillero del Diablo Merlot 2016
DO Valle Central, Chile 13.5% alc. $$

This is a well-priced and attractive merlot that delivers well across the board. The flavours are tangy and concentrated, with good persistence through the palate. They're well balanced by the fresh acidity and the tannins are relaxed and integrated. It's a smart choice for get-togethers over the barbecue or in the kitchen, where you're serving friends red meats, burgers, and seasoned sausages.

Cono Sur 'Bicicleta' Pinot Noir 2016
Chile 13% alc. $$

Cono Sur is Chile's largest producer of pinot noir by far, but the quality is not compromised by the volume. This is a lovely medium-range pinot, with attractive flavours that are consistent and complex right through the palate. The acidity is bright and balanced, and the tannins are integrated. Dry and medium-bodied, it's a wine you can pair with foods as varied as grilled salmon and duck, roast poultry and pork, and medium-strength cheeses.

Cono Sur 'Bicicleta' Cabernet Sauvignon 2016
DO Valle Central 13% alc. $$

It's definitely cabernet sauvignon. This well-priced cabernet delivers very typical flavours that are concentrated, nicely layered, and persistent through the palate. The underlying acid is clean and fresh, and the tannins are drying and easy-going. It's a very easy choice for red meats as well as for grilled sausages and barbecued ribs.

Emiliana 'Coyam' 2013
DO Valle de Colchagua 14.5% alc. $$$

Seven grape varieties contributed to this delicious blend: syrah (48%), carmenère (24%), merlot (11%), cabernet sauvignon (10%), mourvèdre (3%), malbec (3%), and petit verdot (1%). It's a densely flavoured red with plenty of complexity in the fruit, excellent fruit-acid balance, and well-integrated tannins. Drink it with substantial foods such as red meats.

Emiliana Novas Gran Reserva 2015
DO Valle de Colchagua, Chile 14% alc. $$$

Novas is a blend of carmenère (which Chile has adopted as its signature red grape variety) and cabernet sauvignon. It's a really stunning wine that combines authority with poise. There's elegance and structure to the full-on fruit, and it delivers flavours that are layered and focused. The acidity is fresh and clean, giving some welcome juiciness to the texture, and the tannins are moderate. Drink this with red meat-dominant dishes.

Frontera Shiraz-Cabernet Sauvignon 2016
DO Valle Central, Chile 12% alc. $$

[1.5-litre bottle] If you're looking for a well-priced red wine for (a) a party, (b) a backyard barbecue with friends, or (c) to see you through the week (or part thereof), consider this big bottle. The wine shows plenty of attractive fruit that's concentrated and quite complex, clean and fresh acidity, and easy tannins. And a bonus, it's low in alcohol. It's an easy choice for red meats, but will also go with many pork and poultry dishes.

Marques de Casa Concha Cabernet Sauvignon 2015
DO Valle del Maipo 14% alc. $$$

The Maipo Valley, where the vines that produced this wine grow, is Chile's prime cabernet sauvignon region, so you should have high expectations of the wine. You won't be disappointed. It's a lovely, quite elegant cabernet with

CHILE

Concha y Toro. Founded in 1883, Concha y Toro is South America's biggest winery in terms of production. It draws on grapes from its thousands of hectares of vineyards in many of Chile's wine regions. The varieties span the gamut of those grown in Chile, and they're sold under a number of brands. One of the most successful is Casillero del Diablo, named for a wine cellar that (the story goes) the owner told his workers was occupied by the Devil, in order to keep them out. (Visitors to the Concha y Toro estate can visit the cellar, which is now rigged up with diabolical lights and sounds.) Higher tiers of wine include Marques de Casa Concha and Don Melchior.

weighty fruit that's light on its feet. The fruit-acid balance is excellent and the tannins are ripe and moderately gripping. Overall it's a very attractive dry, full-bodied cabernet and it's a great choice for beef and lamb and for rich red meat dishes in general.

Montes 'Alpha' Cabernet Sauvignon 2016
DO Valle de Colchagua 14% alc. $$

This is a delicious cabernet, vintage after vintage. It's from a winery distinctive for it's feng shwei design and cellar where Gregorian chants are played to the barrels. Even if you can't hear them as you pour the wine, you'll enjoy concentrated and well-defined flavours, a mouth-filling texture, balanced acidity, and soft tannins. Drink it with red meats.

Santa Digna Reserva Syrah 2013
DO Valle Central 14% alc. $$

This is identifiably syrah, with some trademark spiciness and pepperiness in the flavour profile. As this suggests, it's complex, and it's also concentrated and well structured. The acid-fruit balance is very good. Dry and medium-bodied, this is a very good choice for many red meats, but the weight and fruit are dialled back enough that it extends easily to richer white meats, as well. Think of roast turkey and pork.

Santa Rita 'Estate Reserve' Carmenère 2016
DO Valle del Rapel 13.5% alc. $$

Once thought to be extinct, carmenère was found thriving in Chile in 1994. Wine producers thought it was a variant of merlot, but once it was identified, carmenère was planted separately and it has become Chile's signature red grape variety. Look for plenty of well-defined fruit flavours in this good example from Santa Rita. It has well-balanced, fresh acidity and negligible tannins. Enjoy it with roasted or grilled red meats.

Santa Rita 'Estate Reserve' Cabernet Sauvignon 2016
DO Valle del Maipo 13.5% alc. $$

The Maipo Valley is Chile's best-known region for cabernet sauvignon, so you should expect quality from this affordable example. It doesn't disappoint. It's definably cabernet sauvignon and has concentrated flavours that are complex and layered, clean and fresh acidity, and tannins that are drying and easy-going. It's an easy wine to pair with red meats, and also extends to poultry and pork dishes.

Santa Rita 'Reserva Especial 120' Cabernet Sauvignon 2016
DO Valle Central 13% alc. $$

This affordable cabernet sauvignon delivers very good quality for the price. You get positive flavours with some complexity and length, the right level of acidity, and relaxed, integrated tannins. It's not a complicated wine, but it's an excellent choice for casual meals of red meat, burgers, grilled sausages, and like dishes.

Undurraga 'Sibaris' Gran Reserva Pinot Noir 2015
DO Valle Leyda 13.5% alc. $$$

The Leyda Valley is one of Chile's cool regions. Close to the Pacific Ocean (which is too cold for swimming off Chile's beaches) the region is blessed with cool breezes and is ideal for pinot noir, as this example shows. The flavours are fine and layered, with decent concentration. The acid is clean and fresh, and the tannins are easy-going. Drink this with poultry and pork, or with mushroom-dominant vegetarian dishes.

CROATIA

Badel Pelješac Plavac Mali 2015
South Dalmatian Coast, Croatia 12% alc. $$

This is 100% made from the plavac mali (pronounced pla-vats mah-lee) variety, which is indigenous to Croatia and related to California's zinfandel and Italy's primitivo. This wine is light-bodied but full of flavour, with good structure, excellent fruit-acid balance, and fairly firm tannins. The style is not unlike many pinot noirs, so bear that in mind when you think of food pairings and drink it with pork, poultry, and red meats.

FRANCE

Albert Bichot Pinot Noir 2015
AOC Bourgogne 12.5% alc. $$

This is one of the classic styles of entry-level pinot noir from Burgundy in an average year. It's on the light side of medium, with fruit that's more intense than the colour suggests it might be. The flavours are bright and quite complex, and they're supported by clean, refreshing acidity. The tannins are dying and easy on the palate. It's a brilliant choice for roast chicken or turkey, for grilled salmon, and for medium-strength cheeses.

Bouchard Père & Fils Bourgogne Pinot Noir 2015
AOC Bourgogne 13% alc. $$-$$$

If you're looking for a stylish red to go with turkey and cranberries, roast chicken, baked ham, or robust summer salads (such as beets), this pinot noir is an excellent candidate. It's made in the understated style often found in Burgundy, with light colour but nicely concentrated flavours, and very good complexity. It's dry, with moderate and manageable tannins, well structured and very well balanced.

Calvet 'Réserve des Remparts' Saint-Émilion 2015
AOC Saint-Emilion 13.5% alc. $$$

This is the sort of wine that makes you appreciate the English love affair with claret—a generic term for red wine from Bordeaux. Saint-Émilion is one of Bordeaux's prestigious appellations, and this merlot-dominant blend shows lovely concentrated and layered fruit, excellent fruit-acid balance, and well-integrated tannins that are still a little grippy. It's an obvious choice for many red meat dishes including, of course, roast beef and Yorkshire pudding.

Carte Noire Côtes du Rhône 2016
AOC Côtes du Rhône 13.5% alc. $$

Mainly grenache and syrah, this is an affordable and attractive Côtes du Rhône that delivers solid flavours and a juicy texture that sets it up for food. Look for decent complexity and concentration in the fruit and good support from the acid, which is clean and fresh. The tannins are relaxed and integrated. This is a versatile wine at the table, where it goes well with red meats and extends to pork and poultry.

C'est la Vie Pinot Noir-Syrah 2016
IGP Pays d'Oc 12.5% alc. $$

Think of this wine, from the south of France, as bridging two regions to the north, with pinot noir (the grape of Burgundy) and syrah (the grape of the northern Rhône Valley). You get the spiciness of syrah here, along with the flavour and acidity of pinot noir. It's not a complicated wine, but it's very drinkable and very versatile with food. You can enjoy it with pork, poultry, and hearty vegetable dishes, as well as with full-flavoured cheeses.

Château Bel-Air Le Bourg 2015
AOC Bordeaux 12% alc. $$

A blend of merlot, cabernet franc, and cabernet sauvignon, this is a classic example of the style of wine that used to be called 'claret'—and still is by some people (mainly older people in Great Britain). The flavours are on the understated side of positive, with good complexity and definition. The acid is correct and fresh, and there's just a little nip from the tannins. It's an excellent wine for roast beef, lamb, or pork.

Château Labarrrade Malbec 2016
AOC Cahors 14% alc. $$

Malbec is the signature grape variety of Cahors, in south-west France. Although the variety is known as cot there, bottles are generally labelled by its more widely recognized name. This well-priced example, sourced from 35-year-old vines, shows quite intense flavours with very good complexity. The acid is fresh and the tannins are moderate. Dry and medium-bodied, it's excellent with red meats and their derivatives, such as burgers and seasoned sausages.

Château Pey la Tour Réserve du Château 2015
AOC Bordeaux Supérieur 15% alc. $$$

A blend that's almost 90% merlot, with some cabernet sauvignon and petit verdot, this is a stylish, almost elegant red that you can happily pair with roast or grilled red meats, braised lamb shanks, and hearty winter stews. It's full of ripe fruit flavours that are positive but not at all overstated, with balanced, clean acidity, and moderate tannins. Overall, it's a very attractive and harmonious red you can keep to the early 2020s if you want to.

Château Puyfromage 2015
AOC Francs Côtes de Bordeaux 14% alc. $$

From the Right Bank in Bordeaux, this wine is predominantly merlot (the main variety in this area) with some contributions from cabernet sauvignon and cabernet franc. It's dry—very dry—and medium-plus in body, and it delivers concentrated flavours with plenty of complexity. The fruit-acid balance is very good, and the tannins still have a little grip, although they're very manageable. Drink it with roasted red meats.

Château Saint-Germain 2016
AOP Bordeaux Supérieur 14% alc. $$

From Bordeaux's Right Bank, this is a blend of merlot and cabernet sauvignon. It's really quite an attractive red, with rich flavours that are well defined, well layered, and that show a good level of structure. All the components are very well balanced and the tannins are drying and perceptible and easily managed. This is an excellent choice for roasted or grilled red meats, including richer game meats.

Château de Vaugelas 'Le Prieuré' 2015
AOC Corbières 14% alc. $$

A blend of grenache, syrah, carignan, and mourvèdre, this is full of ripe, concentrated fruit from attack to finish. It has good complexity and structure, and the acidity shines through the fruit, lightening its depth and providing a texture that verges on juicy. Medium-bodied and dry, it has easy-going tannins and it's a great choice for red meats and well-seasoned sausages.

BEAUJOLAIS REGION, FRANCE

Fat Bastard Merlot 2016
IGP Pays d'Oc 13.5% alc. $$

The Fat Bastard range offers affordable, good-quality wines from the south of France—the Pays d'Oc region that includes some of the areas where Greek settlers first planted wines in Ancient France, two thousand years ago. This merlot gives concentrated fruit flavours with some complexity and definition that are backed by fresh acidity. It's dry and medium-bodied and goes well with red meats and burgers.

Fat Bastard Syrah 2016
IGP Pays d'Oc 13% alc. $$

The story behind the name is recounted on the back label, so you can read it while you drink the wine. It's a bit of a misnomer here, because 'fat' in wine-speak generally means a wine with a relatively low level of acidity—whereas this attractive syrah has acidity that's fresh and complements the well-defined and concentrated fruit. It's medium bodied with drying tannins, and a very good choice for red meats, burgers, grilled sausages, and other such foods.

Georges Duboeuf Beaujolais 2015
AOC Beaujolais 13% alc. $$

This is a bright-flavoured light-to-medium-bodied dry red that delivers well-focused fruity flavours underpinned by fresh acidity. (Don't confuse it with Beaujolais Nouveau, a very young style of Beaujolais that's released for sale in late November.) Made from the gamay variety, this has low tannins and it can be chilled down a little in the summer. Drink it with poultry, pork, and baked ham.

Georges Duboeuf Beaujolais-Villages 2015
AOC Beaujolais-Villages 13% alc. $$

Made from the gamay variety, this is a very dry, medium-bodied red that's very versatile at the table. Think of it for roasted chicken and turkey, for grilled salmon, and for stronger cheeses such as Époisses. The flavours are concentrated and defined, the structure is good, and the spine of acidity is balanced and well calibrated. Beaujolais is too often thought of as being in the fruity style of Beaujolais Nouveau, but this is a totally different animal.

JP Chenet Reserve Cabernet-Syrah 2016
IGP Pays d'Oc 12.5% alc. $$

This red blend isn't going to send you crazy because of its quality, but it achieves exactly what it sets out to do: provide an affordable, well-made, and above all drinkable red wine that's versatile for many occasions. The flavours are concentrated, the acidity is fresh, and the tannins are negligible. It's a good choice when you're having a crowd or just kicking back and grilling some sausages, a burger, or red meat.

JP Chenet Réserve Merlot-Cabernet 2015
IGP Pays d'Oc 13.5% alc. $$

JP Chenet offers a range of well-made, affordable wines from the south of France. As you'd expect of this warm region, it produces wines with plenty of fruit, and you'll find this merlot-cabernet sauvignon blend is one of them. The fruit leads the way here, but not at all aggressively, and it's well supported by fresh acidity. This is a wine you can drink with red meats, grilled sausages, burgers, and ribs.

JP Chenet Réserve Pinot Noir 2016
Vin de France 12.5% alc. $$

This is essentially a fruit-driven pinot noir, with a nice range of ripe flavours identifiable on the palate. They're supported by a seam of fresh acidity, and the tannins are pretty much absent. It's not a complex or astonishing wine, but it's easy-drinking and just the thing for casual get togethers when you're serving burgers, sausages, or ribs.

La Fiole Côtes du Rhône 2015
AOC Côtes du Rhône 13.5% alc. $$

If you know La Fiole's Châteauneuf-du-Pape's weirdly shaped bottle you won't be surprised by the appearance of this Côtes du Rhône. But the wine inside is totally different. This is a full-bodied blend of grenache and syrah that goes very well with grilled red meats. The fruit is full-on, and it's quite well layered and structured. The acid is well balanced and the tannins are soft and integrated.

La Fiole du Pape Châteauneuf-du-Pape
AOC Châteauneuf-du-Pape 13% alc. $$$$-$$$$$

Châteauneuf-du-Pape means 'the pope's new château' and it refers to a place built for Pope John XXII near Avignon in the 14th century. The wine from the local vineyards was first known as 'Avignon wine' but there was more cachet linking it to the papacy, hence the new name. This is a quite elegant red blend (mostly grenache) with great concentration, focus, and balance. The tannins are firm and moderate. Drink it with a rack of lamb or other red meats.

Le Reveil Malbec 2016
IGP Côtes du Lot 12.5% alc. $-$$

Although malbec is now associated with Argentina, its home is in south-west France, along the River Lot, where this one comes from. (It's known as cot, not malbec, there.) This is an easy-drinking example that doesn't have the firm tannins and teeth-staining fruit that many have. Instead you'll find well-concentrated flavours, well-balanced acidity, and manageable tannins. Drink it with red meats, burgers, and grilled sausages.

Les Jamelles Merlot 2016
IGP Pays d'Oc 13% alc. $$

A fairly robust and (in the best sense) slightly rustic merlot from the south of France, this shows quite richly concentrated flavours. They're well layered and they're complemented by a seam of good acidity. It's medium-plus in body and dry, and it's an excellent wine for the summer (or year-round, if you're lucky) barbecue season. Drink it with hamburgers, red meats, sausages, and ribs.

Louis Latour Pinot Noir 2015
AOC Bourgogne 13% alc. $$

This is a reliable Burgundy pinot noir, vintage after vintage. It's medium-weight as pinot noir goes, with nicely concentrated and layered flavours that are supported by fresh, clean acidity. The tannins are soft and well integrated. This is a pinot you can pair equally well with weightier red meat dishes and with lighter meals that feature poultry. It also goes well with quite full-flavoured cheeses.

Marius Grenache-Syrah 2016
IGP Pays d'Oc 13.5% alc. $$

Marius (pictured on the label) was the great-grandfather of Michel Chapoutier, one of France's notable wine producers. This blend from the south of France delivers very attractive flavours that are concentrated and well layered, together with fresh acidity. It's dry with easy-going tannins. Drink it with red meats of all kinds that are prepared in many ways.

Mouton Cadet Rouge 2015
AOC Bordeaux 13.5% alc. $$

Mouton Cadet was established as a brand in the 1950s and has remained one of the most successful French wines since. It's easy to see why, because it delivers very good quality at an excellent price, year after year. This blend (of merlot and cabernets sauvignon and franc) shows lovely concentrated flavours, good complexity, and very good fruit-acid balance. It's dry and medium bodied and goes with red meats, pork, and many hearty dishes.

Ogier 'Héritage' Côtes du Rhône 2016
AOC Côtes du Rhône 14% alc $$

This blend of grenache and syrah is extremely well balanced. On one side of the equation is well-defined fruit that's consistent right through the palate, and on the other is clean, fresh acidity. Although the flavours are quite concentrated, the acidity lightens them up and makes this an excellent partner with food. It works well with red meats and goes equally well with poultry and pork dishes.

Patriarch 'Prestige' Pinot Noir 2015
IGP Pays d'Oc 12% alc. $$

From the warm south of France, you'd expect this to be a bigger, fruitier, and higher-alcohol pinot noir. Instead it's fairly light in body and (as you can see) in alcohol. The flavours are there, though, belying the texture. Overall it's a nicely affordable pinot noir that's well balanced, with good flavour, and a bright, juicy texture. Drink it with grilled salmon, roast chicken and turkey (cranberries will work well), and with medium-strength cheeses.

Pisse-Dru Beaujolais 2016
AOC Beaujolais 12% alc.   **$$**

Red wine from Beaujolais is made from the gamay variety—sometimes called gamay noir. Typically wines labelled simply 'Beaujolais' are dry, fruity, well balanced, and not at all tannic. This one fits the description well and like all gamays it can be served slightly chilled. This goes well with mild cheeses, all kinds of white meat, and salads.

Vive la Vie! Grenache-Syrah-Marselan 2015
Vin de France 12.5% alc.   **$**

Marselan, one of the three grapes that make up this blend, is a little-known variety that's a cross of cabernet sauvignon and grenache. It's gaining in popularity, especially in China. Here it adds to the blend that delivers quite rich flavours with very decent layering. The acidity is well balanced, the wine dry and medium bodied and very inexpensive. It goes well with red meats, pizza, burgers, and with medium-strength cheeses.

GERMANY
Villa Wolf Pinot Noir 2016
Qualitätswein Pfalz 13% alc.   **$$**

This wine is from the company of Ernst Loosen, one of the great names in German wine. It's a pinot noir made in a lighter style, but don't think that makes it inferior. It's dry with flavours that are concentrated and defined, acid that is balanced and juicy, and tannins that are fine and integrated. It's an excellent choice for many pork or poultry dishes (think coq au vin, roast turkey), as well as for grilled trout.

GREECE

Apelia Agioritiko 2016
IGP Peloponnese 12.5% $$

[1.5-litre bottle] Agioritiko, sometimes called St. George, is one of Greece's most planted red grape varieties. Here it's made in a lighter style in terms of weight and body, but it delivers good depth of flavour. The fruit is backed by a seam of bright acidity that gives the texture some juiciness. This is very good value, and the larger format makes it ideal for parties, where it's versatile for many foods, whether red or white meats, fish, or vegetarian.

ITALY

Castello di Gabbiano is located on top of a hill in the Chianti Classico region of Tuscany. Vines grow down the slopes of the hill and Gabbiano produces several levels of chianti that are widely available in Canada. There is also a fine pinot grigio and some higher tiers of red wine, although they have more restricted availability. (Look for Promessa Pinot Grigio and reds such as Alleanza and Bellezza) The castello itself is a fourteenth-century fortified mansion that is now a luxury hotel with a fabulous restaurant. It's an excellent base for touring Tuscany and is very close to Greve in Chianti, an important regional wine town.

ITALY

Barone Montalto
Cabernet Sauvignon-Nero d'Avola 2016
IGT Terre Siciliane 13.5% alc. $-$$

This is a blend of the well-known cabernet sauvignon and the less-known nero d'avola, a grape variety native to Sicily. It's a tremendous bargain at the price. It has plenty of complexity in the concentrated flavours, good fruit-acid balance, and easy-going tannins. This is an excellent red to serve at larger gatherings around a barbecue, and it goes well with red meats, ribs, and seasoned sausages.

Bolla Valpolicella Classico 2016
DOC Valpolicella 12.5% alc. $$

If you're looking for a well-priced Italian wine to go with mid-week tomato-based pasta, this might be the very thing for you. It's a dry, medium-bodied red with bright, serious flavours with a nice level of complexity. The acidity is also bright, bringing some juiciness to the texture, while the tannins are easy going. It's a very good wine for the price, and eminently food-friendly.

Caparzo Sangiovese 2015

IGT Toscana 13.5% alc.   **$$**

Sangiovese is Tuscany's (and arguably Italy's) signature red grape variety and it's used to make wines at all quality and price levels. This is a relatively inexpensive 100% sangiovese, and it brings you the essential qualities of the grape. The flavours are bright, reasonably concentrated and complex, and they're supported by the bright, fresh acidity that's sangiovese's hallmark. This is a great choice for meat or vegetable lasagna and many other tomato-based pastas.

Casal Thaulero Merlot-Cabernet Sauvignon 2016
IGT Terre di Chieti 13% alc.   **$**

Although most Italian wine is made with indigenous grapes, the so-called 'international varieties'—such as merlot and cabernet sauvignon—are widely planted. Here is a well-priced, straightforward blend that delivers a very pleasant and versatile wine. The flavours are solid and persistent and the fruit-acid balance is very good. You needn't drink inexpensive wine only with very casual foods, but this is great with many pizzas and with burgers and grilled sausages.

Cesari Amarone Classico 2013
DOCG Amarone
della Valpolicella Classico 14.5% alc.   **$$$$-$$$$$**

This has all the structure, style, and defined flavours you expect from a well-made amarone. The fruit is deep and broad, with layers of pungent, vibrant, and mature flavours that come on in waves. The texture is rich, tangy, mouth-filling, and surprisingly lively, given the weight of the wine. Dry, full bodied, and delicious, this calls for substantial and well-seasoned red meats such as lamb garnished with mint, and a pepper steak.

Cesari 'Mara' Valpolicella Ripasso Superiore 2015
DOC Valpolicella Ripasso 13.5% alc. $$-$$$

This is a full-bodied, dense red with a mouth-filling and smooth texture that's a good choice when you're grilling well-seasoned red meats, game, or well-seasoned sausages. It has attractive and full-flavoured fruit and plenty of complexity. The tannins are ripe, drying, and have a moderate grip, the acidity is well calibrated to the intensity of the fruit, and there's some distinctive juiciness to the texture—just what you want when pairing it with food.

Citra Montepulciano d'Abruzzo 2015
DOC Montepulciano d'Abruzzo 13% alc. $-$$

It's not a complicated red, but it's well-priced and good quality. The flavours are concentrated and bright, with decent complexity, and they're harnessed to fresh, clean acidity that gives the texture attractive juiciness. Overall, this is very good value, and it goes well with a wide range of dishes that include tomato-based pasta, poultry, and pork.

Citra Sangiovese 2016
IGP Terre di Chieti $

The Citra range of wines offers inexpensive options and general good quality across the board. This sangiovese, for example, gives you plenty of fruit flavours, backed by bright, refreshing acidity. There might not be a lot of complexity or structure, but it's far from many inexpensive reds that tend to be either green or sweet. This goes very well with food, notably pizzas and pastas with tomato-based sauces.

Collavini Merlot 2015
IGT Venezia Giulia 12.5% alc. $-$$

Although we often think of Italian wines as being made from indigenous and local varieties—think of sangiovese, primitivo, and nero d'avola—the so-called 'international varieties' (because they're planted so widely) are very common. Merlot is one, and this is a straightforward, uncomplicated, well-priced example that shows fresh fruit flavours, a degree of complexity, and good acidity. Drink it with casual foods such as burgers and grilled sausages.

Cusumano Nero d'Avola 2016
IGT Terre Siciliane 13.5% alcohol $$

This is one of the few bottles on sale in Canada that has a glass seal. Bear it in mind as you try to unscrew the cap and it doesn't work; you need to remove it to find the glass stopper. It's worth the work, because the wine (made from a grape native to Sicily) is excellent with many red meat and other intensely flavoured dishes. Think of hearty lasagna. The fruit is concentrated and layered, the acid is fresh and clean, and the tannins easy-going.

Cusumano Syrah 2016
IGT Terre Siciliane 13.5% alcohol $$

This is a very affordable syrah that delivers attractive flavours and a spine of acidity that's balanced and fresh. The fruit is quite concentrated, as you'd expect from a Sicilian wine, and it shows good layering and structure, with a little spiciness. The tannins are well integrated and almost imperceptible on the palate. The overall balance of this dry, medium-weight wine is very good, and it's an easy choice for red meats and for medium-strength cheeses.

Doppio Passo Primitivo 2016
IGT Salento 13% alc. $

From the southern Italian wine region of Salento, this wine is made by adding to the fresh grapes some grapes that have been dried. The effect is to give the wine more depth of flavour, and you can taste it here, where the flavours are more concentrated than in conventional wines. At the same time, there's plenty of acidity to balance the fruit, and the tannins are easy-going. Drink this with all-dressed pizza, hearty lasagna, and many red meat dishes.

Fiorini Chianti Superiore 2015
DOCG Chianti Superiore 12.5% alc. $$

This is an impressive chianti for the price. It's made in what might be thought of as a classic style, with lovely complex fruit that's positive and fresh but not too concentrated, plenty of fresh acidity, and just a nip from the tannins. All these features hold together very well, making this an excellent proposition for mid-week pasta with tomato sauce, as well as many chicken dishes and medium-strength cheeses.

Fontanafredda Barolo 2013
DOCG Barolo 14% alc. $$$$

Barolo is a well-loved wine and this is a gorgeous example—one of those winners that delivers power and depth with elegance and style. The flavours are concentrated and well structured, and they're complemented by refreshing and well-calibrated acidity. The tannins are ripe and slightly gripping and this is a great choice if you're having braised lamb shanks or a rich pasta dish in tomato sauce.

Fontella Chianti 2013
DOCG Chianti 12.5% alc. $$

There are many entry-level chiantis on the market, but this is one of those that stand out for quality and value. You'll find very attractive fruit flavours that are concentrated, focused, and consistent from start to finish. The acidity is fresh and clean, and the tannins are ripe and a little firm but easily managed. It's an excellent wine for many red meats, as well as for hearty stews.

Frescobaldi Tenuta di Castiglioni 2015
IGT Toscana 13% alc. $$$

A blend of cabernet sauvignon and merlot, with a little sangiovese and cabernet franc, this is a rich, spicy blend sourced from vineyards south-west of Florence. The flavours are gorgeous, having impressive complexity and structure, not to mention persistence through the palate. The acidity is perfectly calibrated, and the tannins are moderate. Drink this with red meats such as braised lamb shank and Florentine steak.

Gabbiano Chianti 2016
DOCG Chianti 12.5% alc. $$

The Castello di Gabbiano, sitting on a hilltop surrounded by vines, began as a fortified house but is now a boutique hotel. The estate vines produce some excellent wines, including this well-balanced and well–structured chianti. The fruit is bright and layered and the well-calibrated acidity is fresh and clean and gives the texture some juiciness. It pairs well with many Italian dishes, of course, and with red meats generally.

Gabbiano Chianti Classico 2015
DOCG Chianti Classico 13.5% alc. $$-$$$

Chianto Classico is made from grapes growing in the 'classic' region of Chianti, more or less the areas defined as Chianti in the early 1700s. This excellent example from Gabbiano is quite elegant, with well-sculpted flavours, good concentration, and support from a seam of fresh acidity. It's balanced, lightly tannic, and an excellent choice for hearty Italian dishes and red meats in general.

Il Viziato Vino Rosso NV
Italy 13% alc. $$

This is a sangiovese-dominant blend that goes well with red meats, burgers, grilled sausages, ribs ... you get the picture. It's an attractive, somewhat rustic (in a positive sense) red, with a little sweetness in the concentrated and decently complex flavours. It's smooth-textured, with good supporting acidity and is negligibly tannic.

Illuminati Riparosso 2015
DOC Montepulciano d'Abruzzo 13.5% alc. $$

Like many Italian wines, the name includes a grape variety (here it's montepulciano) and a place (Abruzzo). Montepulciano grows in many parts of Italy, but unless it's from Abruzzo, it can't be labelled this way. This is a well-made wine that delivers excellent value. The flavours are complex and well defined and the acidity is balanced and fresh. With integrated tannins, this is an easy choice for veal or pork chops, chicken, and many red meats.

Leonardo Chianti 2015
DOCG Chianti 13% alc. $$

Most chiantis are now bottled in plain bottles, and this is one of the few that still appears in a fiasco—the straw-wrapped tear-drop-shaped bottle that was so popular in the sixties. Then, the bottles were popular because they made fine candle-holders. But let's not get carried away by nostalgia and overlook this wine. It a good chianti, with fresh flavours, decent complexity, and with refreshing, clean acidity. It's great now as it was then: with a plate of spaghetti and meat-balls or a dish of lasagna.

Luccarelli Primitivo 2016
IGP Puglia 13% alc. $

This nicely made primitivo comes from the Puglia region in the heel of the Italian boot—the core production region for primitivo. It's an attractive, slightly rustic (in a positive sense) red that has a lot of fruit, decent complexity, and well-balanced acidity that adds freshness to the texture. It's dry and medium bodied, and very versatile. Drink it with burgers, red meats, hearty pastas, pizza … the list goes on.

Masi 'Bonacosta' Valpolicella Classico 2016
DOC Valpolicella Classico 12% alc. $$

Here's more evidence that you can have low alcohol in a very good quality wine—the level of alcohol that was common in red wines not so long ago. Look for concentrated and high-toned flavours here. They're well defined and focused and supported by fresh, balanced acidity. It's dry and medium bodied with light tannins, and it's a great choice for many pastas, charcuterie, and red meats.

Masi Campofiorin 2013
IGT Rosso di Verona 13% alc. $$$

Made from the corvina, rondinella, and molinara varieties, this is a lovely medium-plus weight red that goes well with red meats and hearty pasta dishes. The flavours are concentrated-to-intense, with excellent definition and layering, and they're supported by clean, refreshing acidity. Potentially full bodied, it's remarkably light on its feet and makes an excellent food wine. It's been a hit ever since the blend was created in the 1960s.

Masi 'Costasera' Amarone Classico 2011
DOCG Amarone Classico 15% alc. $$$$$

Amarone is well known for its intensity and body, which are achieved by drying the grapes before pressing them. This has the effect of reducing the water content and therefore concentrating the flavour compounds in the grapes. It's all very evident in this lovely example that delivers intense flavours and real weight, along with structure and balance. You'll want to pair it with equally intense and weighty food.

Melini Chianti 2015
DOCG Chianti 13% alc. $$

This is a very attractive, well-priced chianti that delivers well across the board. Look for bright flavours that are nicely concentrated and defined, refreshing acidity that gives a touch of juiciness to the texture, and easy-going tannins. Everything's in balance here, and it's an easy wine to pair with any foods. Think of pastas, of course, but also chicken and pork, as well as medium-strength cheeses.

Mezzomondo Negroamaro 2015
IGT Puglia 13% alc. $$

There's some debate about the meaning of this grape variety. It can be translated as 'black and bitter', but producers would understandably rather not have their wines thought of as bitter, and they propose 'black and black' as a better translation. This dry wine certainly isn't bitter. You find quite concentrated, ripe flavours backed by good acidity. The tannins are easy-going and this is an easy choice for many red meats as well as tomato-based dishes.

Monte Antico 2015
IGT Toscana 13% alc. $$

This delicious wine is a blend of sangiovese—the signature red variety of Tuscany—merlot, and cabernet sauvignon. It delivers robust and concentrated flavours that show complexity and depth, with excellent fruit-acid balance. It's dry and medium-bodied, and the tannins are well integrated. It goes well with hearty meat-based pastas, with red meats, and with bold vegetarian food.

Negrar Corvina 2015
IGT Verona 12.5% alc. $

This is a really lovely wine made from the corvina variety. Almost all corvina is grown in the Verona region, and it's usually part of a blend for such wines as Valpolicella and Barolo. Here we have it as a varietal wine that's just medium-bodied and delivers quite high-toned fruit flavours. The texture is bright and juicy, making it an excellent wine for food. This goes well with lighter red meat dishes, pork, poultry, grilled salmon, and medium-strength cheeses.

Piccini Brunello di Montalcino 2012
DOCG Brunello di Montalcino 14% alc. $$$$-$$$$$

Brunello means 'the little brown one', referring to a clone of the sangiovese variety, while Montalcino is the region the wine comes from. These wines are rightfully famous for delivering both weight and style, and this example expresses those qualities well. The flavours are complex, deep, and well defined, and they're perfectly balanced with the clean acidity. The tannins are drying and easy-going. Drink it with red meats, hearty meat-based pastas, and strong cheeses.

Rocca delle Maciè Chianti Classico 2015
DOCG Chianti Classico 13.5% alc. $$

This is a lovely chianti from the 'Classico' region, which more or less covers the area originally designated for chianti centuries ago. Made from sangiovese (95%) and merlot, it's a serious and delicious wine that combines concentrated and well-defined fruit flavour with classic fresh acidity. The tannins are well integrated and the texture is quite dense but light on its feet. This is an obvious choice for the likes of osso buco and hearty pastas, but don't confine it to Italian cuisine, by any means.

Rocca delle Maciè Chianti Riserva 2014
DOCG Chianti Riserva 13.5% alc. $$

Look for concentrated fruit in this very attractive chianti, which is mostly sangiovese with a little cabernet sauvignon and merlot. The flavours are layered and well defined and supported by the fresh acidity you associate with chianti. The tannins are fairly grippy, even now, and a little grainy, but easily managed. This is an excellent choice for red meats, hearty stews, and older, full-flavoured cheeses.

Rocca delle Maciè 'Vernaiolo' Chianti 2016
DOCG Chianti 13% alc. $$

The Chianti wine region produces tens of millions of bottles of wine each year, some of it quite wonderful, much of it very good, and some quite disappointing. This one, from a highly respected producer, definitely belongs in the superior ranks. It shows concentrated flavours or ripe fruit married to juicy acidity. It's dry and moderately tannic, and goes with pork, and lighter red meat dishes in general, not to mention stronger cheeses.

Romio Primitivo 2016
IGT Puglia 13.5% alc. $$

That's Romio, not Romeo. The Italia primitivo variety is very similar to California's zinfandel, and both have been traced back to a Croatian variety. But this is from the warmth of southern Italy, and it shows its provenance in ripe flavours that are quite deep and layered. The acidity gives freshness and sets the wine up for food. Enjoy it with red meats, hearty pastas, and burgers.

Rubesco 2014
DOC Rosso di Torgiano 13.5% alc. $$-$$$

Made by the reliable Lungarotti winery, this is a blend of sangiovese and colorino grape varieties. They add up to a very attractive red with flavours that are quite intense yet light on their feet, thanks to the fresh, bright, and very well-balanced acidity. The tannins are drying and with chimichurri, or roast lamb and mint sauce.

Ruffino 'Aziano' Chianti Classico 2015
DOCG Chianti Classico 13% alc. $$-$$$

This is a very attractive chianti from the original (classico) area delimited as Chianti. By law it must be at least 80% sangiovese, and merlot and cabernet sauvignon are part of the Aziano blend. You'll find the fruit is both serious and bright, with very good complexity and flavour range, while the well-measured acid adds some juiciness to the texture. The tannins have relaxed their grip, and this is a great wine for meats Italian-style.

Ruffino Chianti 2016
DOCG Chianti 12.5% alc. $$

There's something very compelling about chianti wines in general. Typically they deliver good, solid flavours that pair with bright acidity, and they're food wines par excellence. This Ruffino example is no exception. Look for bright, layered, and quite concentrated flavours backed by clean, fresh acidity. It's dry, medium-bodied, and well balanced. It's a natural for many Italian-style dishes, such as pizza and lasagne, as well as red and white meats.

Ruffino 'Il Ducale' 2015
IGT Toscana 13% alc. $$-$$$

Sourced from vineyards near Florence and Siena, this delicious blend is 45% sangiovese, 40% merlot, and 15% syrah. Look for impressive complexity in the flavours, which are concentrated and well defined, and for excellent fruit-acid balance. The tannins are drying and unobtrusive. This is quite elegant and goes very well with osso buco, hearty pastas, and with red meats in general.

Sartori Valpolicella 2016
DOC Valpolicella 12.5% alc. $$

This is a lovely, juicy-textured red blend. Valpolicella is often in this well-measured style, with good fruit concentration, great fruit-acid balance, and easy-going tannins. It really is very drinkable, and it's very versatile at the table. You can enjoy this dry, medium-bodied red with dishes as varied as red meats, poultry, grilled sausages and kefta, and medium-strength cheeses.

Zenato 'Partiale Appassimento' Veneto Rosso 2013
IGT Veneto Rosso 13.5% alc. $$

'Parziale Appassimento' means that the grapes used for this wine were partially dried before they were pressed. This eliminates some of the water and produces more intense flavours. And there they are, concentrated, complex, and well-defined flavours that are supported by a seam of fresh, clean acidity. The tannins are drying and manageable. Drink this with hearty pasta dishes, red meats, and seasoned sausages.

NEW ZEALAND
Kim Crawford Pinot Noir 2016
New Zealand 13.5% alc. $$$

Labelling the provenance as New Zealand, rather than Marlborough or another designated wine region, means that the grapes for this wine were sourced from several locations. In principle such multi-regional blends gain complexity, and that might well be part of the complexity of this pinot noir. It has concentrated and defined flavours, a spine of fresh acidity, and ripe, moderate tannins. Drink it with lamb, pork, and smelly cheeses, such as Époisses.

Oyster Bay Merlot 2016
Hawkes Bay 13.5% alc. $$

Hawkes Bay, on the east coast of New Zealand's North Island has developed a reputation for merlot, so it's not surprising to see a sizable producer like Oyster Bay source this very good merlot from there. It has good depth and breadth of flavour, solid structure, and a very good rapport between the concentrated fruit and the fresh, clean acidity. The tannins are easy-going and this is a good choice for grilled red meats.

Oyster Bay Pinot Noir 2016
Marlborough 14% alc. $$

This is a very attractive pinot noir from a region better known for sauvignon blanc. You'll find delicious flavours that are concentrated, consistent, and quite complex and balanced with fresh acidity. The wine is harmonious, with a refreshing texture that suits it to food, and because it carries more body than leaner styles of pinot noir, it can support weightier dishes such as grilled lamb and beef stews.

PORTUGAL
Altano Douro Red 2013
DOC Douro 13.5% alc. $$

This wine comes from the region where port is made and it contains some of the same grape varieties. As you might expect, it's quite full bodied, with concentrated and well-defined flavours. The acid keeps everything in order and cuts through the weight of the fruit, and the tannins, although drying, are very manageable. This is an excellent choice for many red meat dishes, from steaks to stews.

Catedral Reserva 2015
DOC Dão 13% alc. $$

There's plenty of flavour and a quite rich texture in this affordable blend of three Portuguese grape varieties—all, incidentally, permitted in the production of port. The fruit-acid balance is very good and there's a decent level of complexity in the flavours. The tannins are light. This is a little more than medium in weight, and it pairs well with many grilled or roasted red meats, as well as medium-strength cheeses.

Silk and Spice Red 2016
Portugal 13% alc. $$

This straightforward wine lives up to its name. It's an uncomplicated, well-priced, and easy-drinking red with a smooth texture and a little sweetness. The flavours are full-on fruit and the acidity keeps up well. It might best be drunk on its own, but it also goes well with foods that have a touch of sweetness, such as red meats (such as ribs) with a sweet barbecue sauce or burgers with sweet relish.

Vicente Faria Animus 2015
DOC Douro 13% alc. $$

This is made from three varieties: tinta roriz, touriga nacional, and touriga franca, all grapes familiar to red-wine drinkers in Portugal. It's made in a robust style, with concentrated flavours that are full of ripe fruit. The structure and balance are very good, with clean acidity and drying tannins. This is a natural for red meats, stews, grilled seasoned sausages, and burgers.

SOUTH AFRICA
Fleur du Cap Cabernet Sauvignon 2016
WO Western Cape 14% alc. $$

Almost full-bodied, this is a fruit-filled cabernet sauvignon from the warm growing regions of South Africa. Look for concentrated fruit that's quite complex, support from fresh acidity, and tannins that are drying but unobtrusive. This is an attractive cabernet sauvignon at a very affordable price and it goes well with red meats, burgers, and grilled sausages.

Goats do Roam Red Blend 2016
WO Western Cape 14% alc. $$

Six varieties lent their talents to this wine. The most important are shiraz and cinsault, and the others are grenache, mourvèdre, petite sirah, and carignan. You'd expect some complexity from this sextet, and you won't be disappointed. The flavours are quite lovely—they're concentrated and layered—and they're supported by refreshing acidity. Medium-bodied and dry, this wine goes really well with grilled lamb, and it extends to red meats in general.

STAGS' LEAP WINERY, NAPA VALLEY, CALIFORNIA, UNITED STATES

Nederburg 'The Winemasters'
Cabernet Sauvignon 2016
WO Western Cape 14.5% alc. $$

Nederburg is a big South African producer that turns out many well-made and affordable wines. This cabernet sauvignon shows characters that are quite typical of the variety, with concentrated and quite complex flavours, acidity that's clean and fresh, and pretty relaxed tannins. It's an easy-drinking style of cabernet and equally easy to pair with food. Red meats are obvious, but try it with meat-lovers pizzas and hearty pastas.

SOUTH AFRICA

Goats do Roam is a brand of Fairview winery, which dates back to the late 1600s. The name is a play on Côtes du Rhône, the French wine region, and many of the grape varieties in the Goats do Roam collection are those found in the Rhône Valley. It also reflects the fact that the winery, owned by Charles Back, has a herd of goats, and that on one occasion his young son left the gate open and some of the herd roamed among the vines, eating the grapes, until they were discovered.

Nederburg 'The Winemasters' Shiraz 2016
WO Western Cape 14.5% alc. $$

Wine producers have the option of labelling their wine as syrah or shiraz (as they're the same variety) but it's become usual to use 'shiraz' when it's made in this style: fruit-forward, with concentrated and ripe fruit. This example adds well-balanced acidity. It's medium-bodied and dry, and it goes well with all kinds and preparations of red meats (grilled, braised, roasted, stewed), and casual meals of burgers or ribs.

Thelema Mountain Red 2014
WO Western Cape 14% alc. $$

This is a blend of four main grape varieties—cabernet sauvignon, merlot, petit verdot, and shiraz—with a splash of cabernet franc, and it's been aged 18 months in used barrels. That's a lot of effort for an inexpensive wine, but it shows in the good quality. Look for concentrated and complex flavours, excellent fruit-acid balance, and integrated tannins. It's great for grilled and roasted red meats, hearty stews, and much of the stuff that you barbecue.

Two Oceans Cabernet Sauvignon-Merlot 2016
WO Western Cape 13.5% alc. $$

The two oceans in the name are the Atlantic and the Indian, which meet (the actual meeting-point shifts seasonally) off South Africa's south coast. This is a popular, well-priced blend of 60% cabernet and 40% merlot that shows the depth of cabernet and the fruitiness of merlot. It's a well-made red that's very versatile with food: not so heavy that you can't pair it with pork, for example, yet with the concentration to go with red meats.

SPAIN

Anciano Clásico Garnacha 2016
DOP Valdepeñas 13.5% alc. $$

This is a really lovely garnacha, the Spanish name for the variety more widely known as grenache. It's full of very attractive fruit that's layered with well-defined flavours. The acidity is spot-on in terms of balance and the tannins are easy-going and integrated. This is a pretty versatile wine, and it goes well with richer pork and poultry dishes as well as with red meats.

Anciano '5 Years' Reserva Tempranillo 2010
DOP Valdepeñas 13% alc. $$

The '5 Years' referred to on the label is the minimum aging period of the wine. It's aged at least a year in barrels and the rest of the time in bottles before being released. Made entirely from tempranillo, Spain's signature red grape, this is a delicious red that does well with lighter red meat dishes.

Anciano '7 Years' Gran Reserva Tempranillo 2008
DOP Valdepeñas 13% alc. $$

This tempranillo was aged at least a total seven years in barrel and bottle before being released for sale. Think of it as the producer aging the wine for you and saving you from having to keep it in a cellar. The fruit is concentrated and well layered and the acidity is fresh and clean. The tannins are nicely integrated, and this dry, balanced, and medium-bodied wine goes well with many red and white meat dishes, as well as vegetarian risottos.

Anciano '10 Years' Gran Reserva Tempranillo 2006
DOP Valdepeñas 13% alc. $$

This is an excellent price for a wine already more than ten years old and in excellent condition. If you can pick up its 5 Year and 7 Year siblings, it's a very good way to taste the evolution of a wine. In this one the flavours are still fresh and lively, as is the acidity, while the tannins have integrated almost completely. It's great with many Spanish dishes, and generally pairs well with red meats and richer pork and poultry dishes.

Beau Bonhomme Red 2016
DO Jumilla 14.5% alc. $$

Perhaps it's odd to see a Spanish wine with a French name, but it's made by ex-Montrealer Nathalie Bonhomme. Made in Jumilla in conjunction with the well-known producer, Juan Gil, it's made from the region's signature grape, monastrell (also known as mourvèdre). It's an easy-drinking wine that's full of ripe fruit underpinned by fresh acidity. The high-ish alcohol isn't perceptible. Drink it with paella, grilled chorizo sausage, or a juicy steak.

Beronia Tempranillo Rioja 2015
DOC Rioja 14% alc. $$

Tempranillo is Spain's signature red grape variety and the key variety in Rioja, the country's best-known wine region. Here it makes a high-toned wine with bright, concentrated, and quite complex fruit, underpinned by a seam of fresh, clean acidity. The tannins are drying and moderate and easily approached. This is a very good choice for simple red meat dishes, as well as roast or grilled pork. If you happen to have a pan of paella, it will easily handle that, too.

Beronia 'Elaboración Especial' Tempranillo Rioja 2015
DOC Rioja 14% alc. $$

This is a very juicy-textured tempranillo that's an excellent choice for many lighter red meat dishes as well as poultry and dishes prepared with a tomato base. The flavours are quite concentrated and well layered, the acidity is bright and clean, and the tannins are moderate and drying. Overall, it's an attractive, well-balanced wine.

Beronia Reserva Rioja 2013
DOC Rioja 14% alc. $$$

This is an impressive blend of tempranillo, graciano, and mazuelo, all indigenous Spanish grape varieties. It was aged six years, almost two of them in French and American barrels (the rest in bottle). It's quite elegant in its smooth texture and complex flavour profile, and is shows remarkable freshness for its age. The acidity is right-on—balanced and refreshing—and the tannins are fine and supple. Enjoy it with red meats and with many pork and rabbit dishes.

Castillo de Almansa Reserva 2014
DO Almansa 14% alc. $$

Made from tempranillo, monastrell (aka mourvèdre), and garnacha (aka grenache) grapes, this was aged 12 month in barrels. It delivers concentrated flavours that are spicy and rich, supported by very good acidity. It's dry with a little tannic nip, and it's an excellent choice for hearty meat and vegetarian dishes, as well as with flavourful cheeses such as old cheddar and Époisses.

Gran Feudo Reserva 2012
DO Navarra 13% alc. $$

This is a blend of tempranillo, merlot, and cabernet sauvignon. It's fruit-driven and characterized by good intensity and complexity in the fruit, with a very effective spine of acidity that gives some juiciness to the texture. The tannins are drying and relaxed. This is a great choice for casual meals of red meat and grilled sausages, as well as for stronger cheeses

Hécula Monastrell 2013
DO Yecla 14% alc. $$

Monastrell is the Spanish name for the French mourvèdre—which is also known as mataro in Australia. It's not alone as a grape variety in having many different names. Hécula, on the other hand, is Hécula, a reliable and impressive wine year after year. Look for concentrated-to-intense flavours here, but the wine is light on its feet, thanks to fresh, clean acidity. With easy-going tannins, this is a great match for red meats, hearty pastas, and many paellas.

Honoro Vera Garnacha 2016
DO Calatayud 14.5% alc. $$

Garnacha is a grape variety known as grenache in France and most of the rest of the world, even though Spain has a claim to being its place of origin. It grows in the Mediterranean region (and elsewhere, thanks to global warming) and here it makes a big, robust, rustic (in the good sense) red you'll want to pair with flavourful red meat dishes. It's dry to the point of astringent, and has excellent balance throughout.

Hoya de Cadenas Reserva Tempranillo 2013
DO Utiel Requena 12.5% alc. $$

From a small wine region near Valencia, this is a well-made 100% tempranillo that delivers very good value. The fruit is concentrated and consistent across the palate and shows a nice level of complexity, while the clean acidity is refreshing and well balanced. There's some juiciness to the texture and it's clearly made for food. Drink it with chicken and veal dishes, as well as with mushroom-dominant cuisine.

Liberado Cabernet Sauvignon-Tempranillo 2016
Vino de la Tierra de Castilla 13% alc. $$

This is a straightforward, widely available red blend that's fruity and well balanced and makes for a wine you can sip on its own or pair with foods such as burgers, barbecued ribs, and grilled sausages. There's a little sweetness in the flavours, but it's mostly taken care of by the good acidity. Overall, it's a fairly simple wine but it does its job admirably.

Marques de Riscal Rioja Reserva 2014
DOC Rioja 14% alc. $$

This is a smooth, quite mouth-filling tempranillo-dominant red from Spain's best-known wine region. You can smell and taste a little of the vanilla from the new American oak barrels producers in Rioja have long used, but the fruit remains fresh and bright. The acidity is fresh and clean, and the tannins add to the dryness of the wine but are easy-going. Drink this with grilled sausages and grilled red meats, especially lamb.

Radio Boka Tempranillo 2016
Vino de la Tierra de Castilla 13% alc. $$

This is an entry-level tempranillo that very fairly represents the variety. You'll find plenty of concentrated flavours with decent complexity and good consistency through the palate. The acidity is fresh, clean, and well balanced, and the tannins are relaxed. Drink it with Spanish dishes, such as paella or grilled chorizo sausage, or with lighter red meats and medium-strength cheeses, such as manchego.

Sabor Real Tempranillo 2015
DO Toro 14.5% alc. $$

The Toro wine region is in north-east Spain and critics have been bullish about its wine for years. This very affordable, well-made red is 100% tempranillo and it makes for a flavourful wine that goes well not only with red meats but also with pork and poultry and a host of other dishes. You'll find it has concentrated fruit that's well layered and is nicely balanced by refreshing acidity that gives the texture some juiciness.

UNITED STATES—CALIFORNIA

1000 Stories Zinfandel 2015
California 15.5% alc. $$$

This is a kind of über-zin. Not only does it have very high alcohol and not only is it backed with dark, deep, intense fruit, but it's been aged in barrels that once held Bourbon whiskey. It's a zin for true zin-lovers and a chance for others to taste one of these monsters. For all that, it's well balanced and has plenty of complexity and decent structure. It's not for the faint of heart or faint of food. Drink it with a juicy, well-seasoned, grilled steak or game meat.

Apothic 'Winemaker's Blend' Red 2015
California 13.5% alc. $$

The Apothic line of wines ran into hostility from many wine writers because of their sweetness/fruitiness and low acidity. But they (and other wines in that style) have proved very popular among consumers. This basic red blend is full-bodied and decidedly fruit-forward. It has some tanginess from the acidity, a smooth texture, and slight sweetness from ripe fruit and some residual sugar. It needs food with some weight that's also low in acidity. Unadorned red meats and barbecued ribs would work well.

Apothic Crush Red 2015
California 14.5% alc. $$

Described on the label as a "smooth red blend," this lacks the sweetness of the basic Apothic Red, but has all of its fruit intensity. There's some good complexity to the fruit, and depth to the flavours, and the underlying acidity is well calibrated. There's a little nippy grip to the tannins, but they're fundamentally relaxed. Drink this with seasoned grilled red meats, spicy sausages, and barbecued ribs.

Apothic 'Dark' Red Blend 2015
California 14% alc. $$

The 'dark' refers primarily to 'dark fruit flavours,' says the back label, adding that 'there's a romance in darkness.' Not only are the labels dark (and hard to read), but so is the (artificial) cork. Be all that as it may, this is an intensely flavoured red (undoubtedly with dark fruit flavours), good acid balance, and light tannins. The finish is long. If you plan to eat while drinking this, think of barbecued red meats, with beef and game high on the list.

Barefoot Cabernet Sauvignon NV
California 13.5% alc. $

The Barefoot brand (made by the Gallo company) has been a runaway success—without any support from wine critics. Some wines in the brand are uninteresting, but this cabernet sauvignon has plenty of jammy fruit and the acidity to hold it up. It's essentially dry (with just a touch of residual sugar) and fruity, and it pairs well with barbecued ribs and that sticky sauce, as well as with grilled sausages and burgers.

Beringer 'Founders' Estate' Cabernet Sauvignon 2016
California 13.8% alc. $$-$$$

Beringer is Napa Valley's oldest continuous wine producer, dating back to 1876. It stayed in business during Prohibition by making sacramental wine. This medium-bodied cabernet sauvignon is more delicious than spiritual, however. It has solid and complex flavours backed by clean, juicy acidity, with moderate to easy tannins. It's a very easy choice to pair with red meats and hearty meat stews.

Beringer 'Founders' Estate' Merlot 2016
California 13.8% alc.   **$$-$$$**

Merlot is often overlooked among red wines in cabernet sauvignon-saturated California, but merlot is one of the state's other strong suits. This affordable merlot from Beringer offers lovely fruit flavours that are focused and defined. The acid spine is properly calibrated and the tannins are negligible. Drink it with red meats, pork, and well-seasoned chicken.

Beringer 'Founders' Estate' Zinfandel 2016
California 14.4% alc.   **$$-$$$**

You really couldn't have a line of California red wines without a zinfandel, the variety that has become closely identified with the state. This example delivers what you expect of the variety: plush, quite dense fruit flavours, fairly high alcohol, and good balance. Overall it's a very successful zin, with good structure and balance. It's dry, medium-plus in weight, and has soft tannins, and it's ready to go whenever you put some grilled red meat on your plate.

Beringer Knights Valley Cabernet Sauvignon 2015
Knights Valley 13% alc.   **$$$$$**

This is a stunning cabernet sauvignon, vintage after vintage. It achieves the feat that distinguishes many fine wines of being both bold and stylish at the same time. The flavours are deep, broad, and intricately layered, the texture is plush and generous, and the acidity is tailored to the fruit. It's full-bodied and the tannins are still gripping—you can easily hold this for five to ten years from the vintage. Enjoy it with a juicy sirloin steak.

Beringer 'Main & Vine' Cabernet Sauvignon 2017
California 13% alc. $$

The label states that the flavours are 'jammy', which is not usually much of a recommendation. I'd say they were concentrated and ripe and on the virtuous side of the jammy line. There's good structure to this affordable cabernet, along with well-balanced acidity and easy-going tannins. It's a very good choice for many red meats, as well as burgers and well-seasoned sausages.

Bonterra Cabernet Sauvignon 2016
California 13.8% alc. $$

Made from organically grown grapes, this is a very attractive cabernet sauvignon from an environmentally sound winery. (Even the label is made from 100% recycled materials.) You'll find the fruit flavours concentrated and defined, with good complexity and true to the variety. The acidity is very well balanced and the tannins are relaxed. Enjoy this with red meats, burgers, and grilled sausages.

Canyon Road Cabernet Sauvignon 2016
California 13% alc. $$

This is one of the least-expensive cabernet sauvignons on the market, and it tastes like a cabernet sauvignon, not just a generic red wine. Look for fairly concentrated and complex fruit that's backed by clean acidity. The tannins are integrated and hardly evident. This is a good wine for casual, mid-week meals of pasta, beef or pork fajitas, or pork chops, and it's an affordable choice for get-togethers around the barbecue.

Carnivor Cabernet Sauvignon 2015
California 14.5% alc. $$

It's hardly necessary to say that this is a wine built for meat-lovers, even if the name lacks the final 'e'. It's a big-boned, full-bodied, full-fruit red of the kind often called a fruit-bomb. But it's not one of those: it has decent acid supporting the intense fruit flavours, and if the acidity's not high, it's balanced. It's just that the fruit is so intense. As for the meat, steak is the first thing that comes to mind, but richer game meats are also obviously in the picture.

Chateau St-Jean Pinot Noir 2016
California 13.5% alc. $$-$$$

It's hard to find a wine made by Chateau St-Jean that doesn't speak the language of quality, and this pinot noir is no exception to the rule. The flavours are focused, well defined, and elegant, and they're in perfect harmony with the fresh acidity that supports them. The tannins are fine and integrated, and the overall effect is harmonious. It's versatile enough to pair with rich seafood (try lobster), roast chicken and pork, and grilled lamb.

Fetzer 'Valley Oaks' Cabernet Sauvignon 2016
California 13.5% alc. $$

This is a well-made cabernet sauvignon that shows concentrated and quite complex flavours that are reasonably restrained yet solid right through the palate. The fruit-acid balance is very good, and the tannins are light. It's dry and medium-bodied, and goes very well with red meats but it has the lightness of touch to pair nicely with pork and richer poultry dishes.

Fetzer 'Eagle Peak' Merlot 2015
California 13.5% alc. $$

Fetzer early earned a reputation not only for making quality wine but also for doing it in ways that were environmentally responsible. In this sense they were well ahead of the pack. This is a fairly robust merlot that shows solid, complex fruit flavours, good structure, and very good fruit-acid balance. The tannins are quite firm but very manageable. It's a natural for red meats of all kinds.

First Press Cabernet Sauvignon 2015
Napa Valley 14.5% alc. $$$

Napa Valley and cabernet sauvignon go together as naturally as Mendoza malbec and Marlborough sauvignon blanc. This is a fairly mainstream example, which is anything but a bad thing. The fruit—which is big and drives the wine—is defined and decently structured, and there's good fruit-acid balance. The tannins are there, but they're quite easy-going. This is a wine that really needs big food if it's not to dominate. Think steak and game meats.

Ghost Pines 'Winemaker's Blend' Merlot 2015
Sonoma County/Napa County 14.5% alc. $$$

This is one of those blends that brings together not different varieties, but grapes of the same variety from different regions—thus different qualities. It's a lovely merlot that shows quite intense flavours with very good layering. The acidity is very well balanced and the tannins are drying and easily managed. Overall it's very harmonious and is a good pairing for red meats and rich stews and pasta dishes.

Gnarly Head Old Vine Zinfandel 2015
Lodi 14.5% alc $$

There's no definition of 'old' in 'old vines' but there are some very old zinfandel vines (over 100 years old) in California. The point of labelling a wine that way is that older vines produce grapes with more concentration, and you can see that in this densely flavoured zinfandel. That said, there's good complexity, structure, and definition to the wine, and the fruit is balanced by clean acidity. Still, it's a weighty number and it needs food with robust flavours and texture, such as well-seasoned red meats.

Ironstone Old Vine Zinfandel 2016
Lodi 14.5% alc. $$-$$$

This is a richly flavoured and densely textured zinfandel that goes well with weightier and full-flavoured foods such as well-seasoned red meats and steaks with sauces. The flavours are deep and broad, with fruit-sweetness at the core, and the well-balanced acidity does its work of moderating the density of the fruit. The tannins are easy-going. Overall, it's a remarkably drinkable wine, given its weight and intensity, but it does need food.

J. Lohr 'Los Osos' Merlot 2015
Paso Robles 13.5% $$$

Los Osos might refer to bears or to a small coastal community near Paso Robles, where this wine is made. Either way, this is a lovely merlot that delivers plush, concentrated flavours with both depth and breadth. Despite the weight of the fruit, it has a fresh texture, thanks to a seam of clean acidity, while the tannins are medium and manageable. This is a robust merlot that calls for robust food, such as steak and other red meats.

Josh Cellars 'Josh' Cabernet Sauvignon 2015
California 13.5% alc. $$-$$

This is a big, robust cabernet sauvignon that's packed with ripe fruit flavours. It has the heft you associate with California cabernet but it's an approachable wine, not the sort that tires your palate after a single glass. Look for good layering in the fruit, acidity that's well calibrated, and easy-going tannins. That said, it's still a big wine and it needs big food if it's not to dominate your meal, so serve it with well-seasoned red meats.

Josh Cellars 'Josh' Legacy Red Blend 2016
California 14% alc. $$-$$$

This is a big-bodied red blend that shows a hint of sweetness. It delivers full-on fruit with flavours that are pretty complex, a texture that's round, smooth, and mouth-filling, and a good level of acidity. The tannins are negligible. A juicy steak, especially seasoned with steak spices, wouldn't go amiss with this, and neither would lamb and richer game meats.

Kendall-Jackson 'Vintner's Reserve' Cabernet Sauvignon 2014
Sonoma County 13.5% alc. $$$

This is a stylish cabernet sauvignon that goes very well with all kinds of red meat—game, beef, lamb—whether grilled or roasted. The fruit here is really lovely. It's plush and full-flavoured without crossing the line to jammy, and it's layered and defined. The clean and fresh acidity keeps up easily, and the tannins are ripe and soft. It's somewhere between medium and full in body and extremely well balanced.

Kendall-Jackson 'Vintner's Reserve' Pinot Noir 2016
Califiornia 14.5% alc. $$$

Pinot noirs span a spectrum from light-bodied to almost full-bodied, from savoury flavours to sweet. This one sits somewhere in the middle, making it a versatile wine with food. Medium-bodied and dry, it shows attractive flavours of ripe fruit that are concentrated and well layered. The acidity is bright and clean, and the tannins drying and easy-going. It has the weight to go with red meats, and the lightness to go with chicken and pork.

La Crema Pinot Noir 2016
Monterey 13.5% alc. $$$-$$$$

La Crema's pinot noirs are among California's finest. This one is from Monterey, about halfway between San Francisco and Los Angeles, and it's a beauty. Look for nuanced fruit flavours that are substantial and yet light on their feet, married to fresh, clean acidity that contributes some juiciness to the texture. Overall it's an elegant wine that goes well with grilled or roasted duck and lamb.

Liberty School Cabernet Sauvignon 2014
Paso Robles 13.5% alc. $$$

Paso Robles, located between San Francisco and Los Angeles, has emerged as a quality wine region. The Hope family, which makes Liberty School, is one of the key producers, and here they deliver a well-made, very drinkable cabernet sauvignon. The flavours are concentrated and focused and the acid is fresh and correctly balanced. With integrated tannins, this makes a good choice for red meats and burgers.

Louis M. Martini Cabernet Sauvignon 2014
Napa Valley 15.5% alc. $$$-$$$$

Napa Valley has a reputation for making cabernet sauvignon in a robust, full-on fruit style—the style implied by the words 'Napa Cab'. This is one of them. It's full-bodied and big-boned with fruit that's intense and deep in flavour. At the same time, it has good structure and the acid-fruit balance is very good. Unlike some Napa Cabs, this won't kill any nearby food, but you should still pair it with heavier, full-flavoured dishes such as well-seasoned steak.

Louis M. Martini Cabernet Sauvignon 2015
Sonoma County 13.5% alc. $$$

This is a full-bodied, fruit-forward cabernet, but don't think of it as a fruit-bomb. It's well structured and balanced, with a seam of clean, fresh acidity effectively offsetting the intensity of the fruit. The tannins are drying but easy-going. There's a lot of complexity here, too, and this is a wine you can pair easily with straight steak or with meat that's been seasoned or comes with peppercorn or some other sauce.

Meiomi Pinot Noir 2016
Monterey County, Santa Barbara County,
Sonoma County 13.7% alc. $$$

This is a full-bodied pinot noir with full-on fruit, making it a different style from most. The flavours are rich and layered with a hint of sweetness, the texture is smooth and opulent, the fruit-acid balance is good, and the tannins are soft. This style calls for fairly robust food such as a juicy ribeye steak.

Ménage à Trois 'Midnight' Dark Red Blend 2016
California 13.5% alc. $$

Look for bold, rich flavours ... actually, you don't need to look for them—they'll come looking for you. This is one big red wine, with heady, mouth-filling flavours. There's a touch of sweetness, but this isn't a sweet wine—in fact, the acidity takes care of most of it. The weight of the wine makes it tricky to pair with food, but if you want to, think of steak and other red meats.

Murphy Goode Cabernet Sauvignon 2014
California 13.5% alc. $$$

Here's another excellent cabernet sauvignon from California. Little wonder that the variety and the state are so easily associated in the term, 'California cab'. Speaking of cabs, California has a reputation for Uber-the-top wines, but this isn't one. The flavours are positive and well measured, with complexity and structure. The acid is balanced, and the tannins tamed. It's a terrific wine for steaks and burgers.

Pepperwood Grove Old Vines Zinfandel 2015
California 14% alc. $$

There's no agreed-upon definition of how old vines must be before they can be called 'Old Vines' but clearly these are old in someone's mind. Whatever their age, they've produced a very attractive zinfandel that's much more drinkable and versatile than many. The flavours are nuanced and although they're concentrated, they're not in your face and they're supported by good, clean acidity. Drink this with red and white meats.

Ravenswood 'Old Vine' Zinfandel 2015
Lodi 14.5% alc. $$-$$$

Zinfandel is quite often high in alcohol, with some running over 16%. High alcohol isn't an issue as long as you know what you're drinking—and as long as you can't smell or taste it in the wine. No danger of that here. This is a gorgeous, rich zinfandel with a plush texture, defined flavours that go on and on, and well-calibrated acidity. It's a weighty wine and it demands weighty food if it's not to overpower your meal. Think of well-seasoned red meats and game.

Ravenswood 'Vintner's Blend' Zinfandel 2015
California 13.5% alc. $$-$$$

This is a well-paced zinfandel with good structure and balance and made to go with food. Look for concentrated flavours that show some depth and complexity and that hold solid right through the palate. The underlying acidity is well balanced and the drying tannins are well integrated. This is an excellent partner for red meats—think of steak, with or without sauce—and for richer foods such as barbecued ribs with tangy sauce.

USA—CALIFORNIA
Robert Mondavi wines are probably well known to almost all wine drinkers. Robert Mondavi was a pioneer and critical influence on the development of the modern California wine industry. Wines carrying his name are popular across Canada—as are wines from the company that do not carry his name, such as the Woodbridge brand. Besides the California work-horse grapes—chardonnay and cabernet sauvignon—Mondavi notably makes Fumé Blanc, a fine barrel-aged sauvignon blanc. But the best-known are the reds such as Robert Mondavi Napa Valley Cabernet Sauvignon and Robert Mondavi Knights Valley Cabernet Sauvignon.

Robert Mondavi Maestro 2014
Napa Valley 14.5% alc.   **$$$$$**

This is an impressive blend that's about three-quarters cabernet sauvignon, a quarter cabernet franc, and small parts of merlot and petit verdot—a Bordeaux blend, in effect—from various sites in Napa Valley. It's a beautiful wine that combines power with finesse. Look for broad and deep flavours, excellent fruit-acid balance, and ripe, integrated tannins. Bold and finely structured, it calls for flavourful, weighty food such as a juicy ribeye steak.

Robert Mondavi Napa Valley Cabernet Sauvignon 2014
Napa Valley 15% alc.   **$$$$-$$$$$**

This is a big-bodied and impressively structured wine that is mostly (86%) cabernet sauvignon, with support from merlot (10%), petit verdot, cabernet franc, malbec, and syrah. The flavours are deep and layered and the fruit is well supported by clean, clear acidity. The relatively high alcohol is imperceptible on the nose or palate. This is a wine for substantial fare. Beef and lamb are obvious choices.

Robert Mondavi 'Private Selection' Cabernet Sauvignon 2016
California 13.5% alc.   **$$**

The 'Private Selection' series delivers quality and value, and this cabernet sauvignon fits into the range effortlessly. The flavours are concentrated and nicely layered and the texture is generous and smooth, while retaining freshness from the acidity. The tannins are firm and manageable. This is a natural for grilled or roasted red meats, and it extends to rich pasta dishes and to aged cheddar cheese.

Rodney Strong Pinot Noir 2015
Russian River Valley 14.5% alc. $$$$$

The Russian River Valley in the south of Sonoma County is prime pinot noir real estate because the fog that swirls up the valley each days cools the area and produces the conditions in which pinot thrives. This is a really lovely example, with concentrated, focused, and nuanced fruit balanced by fresh, clean acidity. With light-moderate tannins, it's quite elegant and makes an excellent partner for grilled lamb or duck breast.

Sledgehammer Cabernet Sauvignon 2016
California 13.9% alc. $$

With a name like this, you'd expect the wine to be anything but subtle and delicate. And you'd be right. At the same time it's not just a blunt object because although it's full-bodied, robust, and chock full of ripe fruit flavours, there's structure here and the acidity clicks in to lighten the fruit. Still, weighty food is called for, and you might think of steak with some kind of sauce or seasoning—Montreal steak seasoning or a peppercorn sauce, for example.

Smoking Loon Cabernet Sauvignon 2015
California 13.5% alc. $$

This is a popular cabernet sauvignon because it delivers the essence of what many people look for in the variety. The fruit is solid and consistent from start to finish and the flavours are concentrated and decently complex. The acidity is clean, fresh, and balanced, and the tannins are easy-going. It's an attractive medium-bodied red and very versatile with food. Drink it with casual burgers and ribs or pair it with beef or lamb.

Sterling 'Vintner's Collection' Cabernet Sauvignon 2015
California 13.5% alc. $$

Cabernet Sauvignon is widely thought of as California's red grape, even though many other varieties are grown in the state. Still, it's a place to look if you want a fruit-driven cabernet with concentrated flavours and overall balance. It is one such wine. Look for nicely defined fruit with underlying acidity that's clean and fresh. The classic cabernet tannins are muted here, and it's ready to roll with red meats, grilled sausages, and barbecued ribs.

Sterling 'Vintner's Collection' Merlot 2015
California 13.5% alc. $$

This is a very juicy textured merlot with measured and good acidity that set it up to go well with a wide range of foods, from steak and hearty stews to mushroom risotto and coq au vin. This is not an in-your-face California merlot, but one that shows good restraint and structure, with layered flavours and fresh acidity. The tannins are well integrated.

Sterling 'Vintner's Collection' Pinot Noir 2016
California 13.5% alc. $$

Look for a fruit-driven pinot noir in this bottle, with ripe-sweet flavours that are quite dense and concentrated. There's good complexity, the fruit-acid balance is good, and the tannins are easy-going. Overall it's a weightier pinot noir than many, but the flavours are identifiably pinot. Its weight suits it to heavier dishes, including beef and lamb, and it also goes well with hearty meat stews.

Stone Cellars Cabernet Sauvignon 2015
California 12.5% alc.   **$$**

This is a very decent, straightforward cabernet sauvignon that's unpretentious and well made. It's dry and medium-bodied, and has good cabernet flavours in the focused fruit. It has fresh, clean acidity and light tannins and it's overall an attractive, easy-drinking wine. Red meats are obvious partners, of course, as are burgers, ribs, sausages, and the like.

Tom Gore Cabernet Sauvignon 2015
California 13.5% alc.   **$$-$$$**

This is a quite stylish cabernet sauvignon with flavours that are forward and positive, layered and structured. It's far from the crass fruit-bomb style of cabernet you sometimes find from warm regions. As if to reinforce this, the acidity is fresh and well tailored to the fruit, and the tannins are ripe and moderate. Red meats are the obvious food pairing—a juicy steak and this would be wonderful—and it also goes with hearty stews and gourmet burgers.

Wente 'Southern Hills' Cabernet Sauvignon 2015
Livermore Valley, San Franciso Bay 13.5% alc.   **$$-$$$**

Full bodied, well structured, and plush, this is a cabernet sauvignon in the best California tradition. There are indeed cabs from California that are over-the-top in fruit, weight, and alcohol, but this isn't one of them. Here the components—complex fruit, fresh acidity, light tannins—are in excellent balance and ready for the food you set down beside the glass. Red meats are obvious, but hearty pastas and stews work, too.

Wente 'Riva Ranch' Pinot Noir 2014
Arroyo Seco, Monterey 14.5% alc. $$$-$$$$

This is beautiful fruit-driven pinot noir that shows quality right through. The flavours are complex, focused, and high-toned, and they're complemented by perfectly calibrated acidity. The tannins are well integrated. This is a quite elegant pinot that you can enjoy with many poultry and pork dishes. But coq au vin springs to mind.

Z. The Seven Deadly Zins 'Old Vine' Zinfandel 2015
Lodi 15% alc. $$$

Made by Michael David, this is a classic zinfandel that's packed with flavour and carries a hefty level of alcohol. From a tasting and drinking perspective, though, the important thing is that the alcohol is imperceptible. Overall the wine is well balanced with the acidity meeting the full-on fruit at a happy point. This is a big wine for big food, so think of well-seasoned red meats or well-sauced barbecued ribs.

UNITED STATES—WASHINGTON
Columbia Winery Cabernet Sauvignon 2015
Columbia Valley 13.7% alc. $$-$$$

This is an attractive style of cabernet sauvignon, with a higher level of acidity than found in many. This reflects Washington's cooler growing conditions that promote the development of acids in the grapes and produce a wine that's friendly to food. The flavours are concentrated and complex and well balanced with the acid, while the tannins are relaxed. It's a no-brainer to pair this with red meats, and also with sausages and burgers.

Columbia Crest 'Grand Estates' Cabernet Sauvignon 2015
Columbia Valley 13.5% alc. $$

Columbia Crest makes a very reliable, good quality line-up of wines, and this cabernet sauvignon fits in just perfectly. You'll find it has very attractive concentrated fruit with plenty of complexity. It's backed by a well-calibrated seam of clean acidity that gives some juiciness to the texture and suits it to food. With easy-going tannins, this is a great choice for red meats of all kinds.

H3 Cabernet Sauvignon 2015
Horse Heaven Hills 14.5% alc. $$-$$$

Made by the Columbia Crest winery, this is sourced from the unusually named Horse Heaven Hills wine region. Look for breadth and depth in the concentrated flavours, with nice structure and persistence. The acidity supports the fruit very well, while the tannins are light to moderate. It's robust enough to demand fairly flavourful and weighty food which might include steak, grilled lamb, or juicy burgers.

The Velvet Devil Merlot 2015
Washington State 13.5% alc. $$-$$$

It's a pretty bold label—unadorned, all-caps, black on white, with an image of a pitchfork—for a pretty bold wine. This is a fruity number (666?) with big flavours, decent complexity, and good fruit-acid balance. It's dry and medium-plus in body and the obvious food pairing is red meat. But think of red meat in its many incarnations (so to speak): burgers, empanadas, pies, sausages, and so on.

BAROSSA VALLEY, SOUTH AUSTRALIA, AUSTRALIA

Wine
is the only
artwork
you can drink.

- LUIS FERNANDO OLIVERRI

ROSÉ WINES

Astica Rosé 2016
Mendoza 12.5% alc. $

Malbec is Argentina's signature red grape variety and the great bulk of it is used to make full-flavoured red wines. But here we find it as a dry, medium-weight rosé that you can drink on its own or, better still, drink it with lighter foods. Many chicken and pork dishes go well with this wine, which has bright, fresh flavours and crisp, drying acidity that's well tailored to the fruit.

CANADA—BRITISH COLUMBIA

Road 13 'Honest John's' Rosé 2017
BC VQA British Columbia 13.8% alc. $$

Merlot and gamay noir make up 90% of the blend, with viognier, syrah, pinot noir, and cabernet franc (at 0.5%) combining to add the final 10%. Ignoring the trend toward pale-hued rosés, the electric pink of this one makes a bold statement, and the wine itself is bolder in flavour and texture than many rosés, but it maintains balance and freshness. Drink it with salade niçoise, roast poultry and pork, or enjoy it on its own.

See Ya Later Ranch 'Nelly' Rosé 2016
BC VQA Okanagan Valley 13.5% alc. $$

This rosé is a blend of two red varieties (merlot and gamay) and one white (gewürztraminer). The result is a bright dry, medium-bodied wine with plenty of flavour and very good complexity. The acidity is crisp and clean and the wine is very harmonious. You can certainly drink this on its own, but it also goes very well with food. Think of chicken and pork dishes, charcuterie and patés, and also grilled sausages.

CANADA–ONTARIO
Pelee Island Cabernet Franc Rosé
VQA South Islands, Ontario 12.5% alc. $$

This is a very attractive orange-pink rosé that's 100% cabernet franc. It's a fairly serious rosé in terms of its flavours. There's a touch of sweetness, but it's essentially dry, and the flavours are focused and consistent. The acid is well calibrated, and there's some juiciness to the texture. This is a terrific wine for poultry, grilled salmon, and salade niçoise.

CHILE
Casillero del Diablo Reserva Rosé 2017
DO Central Valley, Chile 13% alc. $$

The colour is the very pale pink that's popular among rosés. The fruit is well done: quite delicate but concentrated enough to be very tasty, with a flavour profile that's focused and defined. The acid is managed excellently: it's crisp and clean and, although you can easily sip this rosé on its own, the acidity makes this a good aperitif. Or take it straight to the table, where it goes well with chicken, pork, and many salads.

Cono Sur Pinot Noir Rosé 2017
DO Valle del Bio Bio 13% alc. $$

Cono Sur is Chile's largest producer of pinot noir, so it's not surprising to see a rosé made from the variety. Made from grapes grown in one of the country's most southerly and cool wine regions, this is full of lovely fresh fruit flavours that are defined and layered. The crisp acidity plays to the fruit, making for a refreshing rosé you can drink on its own or pair with chicken, pork, and seafood salads.

Errazuriz Cabernet Sauvignon Rosé 2017
DO Valle Central 12% alc. $$

Rosé is said to be the only wine that people buy 'with their eyes', because colour is so important. It's the reason most rosés are sold in clear glass bottles. This is not the popular very pale pink, but it's a delicious dry rosé that's medium-bodied, crisp-textured, and well balanced. You can drink it with grilled salmon, white fish, seafood, and many salads, like a warm goat cheese salad.

FRANCE

Gérard Bertrand 'Côte des Roses' Rosé 2016
AOP Languedoc 12.5% alc. $$

This really lovely rosé is a blend of grenache, cinsault, and syrah. Fashionably and deceptively pale in colour, it delivers anything but pale flavours. It's full of bright, well-layered fruit that's well supported by crisp, clean acidity. This is a dry rosé that you can well drink on its own, but it's excellent with food. Try it with chicken burritos and salads of many kinds.

Rosé wines have finally entered the mainstream of wine consumption. Formerly considered frivolous sweet wines, 'women's wine', and suitable only for summer, they now come in many styles and are widely drunk throughout the year. France led the way: about three in every ten bottles of wine consumed there are rosé, and rosé wine production and consumption are rising everywhere. The new generation of rosés is mainly dry, sourced from vines dedicated to rosé production, and pale in colour. The key region of production is Provence, in south-east France, but rosé wines are now made throughout the wine-producing world from many different grape varieties.

Pink Gecko Rosé 2016
AOP Coteaux Varois en Provence 12.5% alc. $$

Provence, in south-east France, is associated with rosé wine like no other region in the world. The wines are made in a range of styles, and this is a very attractive one. It's light pink, like so many rosés from the region, is dry and a little fruity, and has very good acidity—just the right level for juiciness and freshness. Enjoy it with poultry, salads, and mild-flavoured cheeses.

NEW ZEALAND

Kim Crawford Rosé 2017
Hawkes Bay 13.5% alc. $$

Made almost entirely (99%) from merlot, with a soupçon of syrah, this is an attractive and popular rosé for year-round drinking. It's dry and has substantial weight, which means it will pair well with more substantial dishes, and the layered fruit is well balanced by the acidity. Drink it with poultry and pork, as well as salmon, white fish, and seafood.

SPAIN

Gran Feudo Rosado 2016
DO Navarra 13% alc. $$

Made predominantly from garnacha, with a little help from tempranillo and merlot, this is a dry and well-balanced rosé (rosado, in Spanish). It's not too complicated, but there's a little complexity to the fruit flavours and the acidity clicks in nicely to provide a refreshing texture. It's a very drinkable wine, one you can enjoy on its own or pair with dishes such as salads and roast chicken and pork.

Beringer 'Main & Vine' White Zinfadel 2016
California 10% alc. $-$$

White zinfandel is typically a lightly to moderately sweet wine made, of course, from the zinfandel variety—which is usually used to make full-bodied and often high-alcohol red wines. White zin (as it's generally called) has been a top-seller in the US, although sales are now declining. This example offers slightly sweet, fresh and fruity flavours, with a little complexity. The acid-fruit balance is good. Drink it on its own or with slightly sweet food.

Meiomi Rosé 2016
Sonoma County, Monterey County,
Santa Barbara County 13.2% alc. $$$

This is a fairly full-bodied and essentially dry rosé that's dressed in medium-pink. It's well balanced, with the well-defined fruit complemented by crisp, clean acidity. It's made mainly from pinot noir and that's reflected in the flavours and texture. This is an excellent choice for roast turkey (with cranberries—think of it for Thanksgiving) and poultry in general.

In victory
you deserve
Champagne.
In defeat,
you need it.

- NAPOLEON BONAPARTE

SPARKLING WINES

Toso Chardonnay Brut Sparkling Wine NV

Mendoza 12.5% alc. $$

Made from 100% chardonnay by Pascual Toso, this is a perky sparkling wine that delivers solid fruit flavours from start to finish, along with bright, fresh acidity. The bubbles are plentiful and persistent, and it's a versatile wine that you can sip on its own, drink as an aperitif with a range of appetizers, or bring to the table with many chicken and pork dishes.

AUSTRALIA

Jip Jip Rocks Sparkling Shiraz NV

South Eastern Australia 13% alc. $$

Sparkling shiraz isn't everyone's cup of tea. You can love shiraz and love sparkling wine, but not love sparkling shiraz. Even so, it has a compelling character, perhaps because it is an unlikely combination, and Australians do it very well. The flavours here are pure shiraz—all dark fruit, some sweetness, and good complexity—but the acidity is higher and there are (of course) the bubbles. You can sip it on its own or pair it with red meats.

Benjamin Bridge Méthode Classique NV

Nova Scotia 11% alc. $$$-$$$$

Benjamin Bridge not only set the bar high for sparkling wines from Nova Scotia, but produces some of Canada's best fizz. This one is made from l'acadie blanc, vidal, chardonnay, seyval, and pinot noir, and it's really delightful. Look for defined flavours, zesty acidity, and loads of bubbles. It's terrific as an aperitif and at the table with fish, seafood, and white meats.

Benjamin Bridge Brut Reserve 2012

Nova Scotia 11% alc. $$$$$

This is Benjamin Bridge's top tier sparkling wine, and it's a beauty. It's made in the Classic Method from chardonnay (65%), pinot noir (25%), and pinot meunier (10%), a blend that here produces finesse and elegance. The flavours are focused and defined, the acidity is perfectly calibrated, and the bubbles emerge as fine beads. You can cellar this five, ten, or more years. Or drink it now with white meats and fish prepared in a cream sauce, like escalopes de veau or poulet.

Benjamin Bridge Pétillant Naturel 2017

Nova Scotia 11% alc. $$$$

Pétillant Naturel wines (often called 'pet nat') are lightly sparkling and are made by bottling the wine during fermentation. It thus finishes fermentation in the bottle (creating the bubbles) and throws a small deposit of dead yeast cells. This example from Benjamin Bridge is really lovely, with rich fruit flavours, bright acidity, and light and persistent fizziness. There's some light fruity-sweetness that makes it perfect for drinking on its own or for pairing with spicy Asian cuisine.

Cave Spring Blanc de Blancs Brut NV
VQA Niagara Escarpment 12% alc. $$$

Made from chardonnay, this is a very well-made sparkling wine that delivers on all fronts. It shows terrific fruit flavours that complement the clean, zesty acidity, and it delivers streams of fine bubbles. You can enjoy this on its own any time of day or night, throughout the year, as an aperitif, or with many foods, including white meats and seafood.

Château des Charmes Brut Sparkling Wine
VQA Niagara-on-the-Lake 12.5% alc. $$$

Made by the Traditional Method (the method used to make champagne) this is a blend of pinot noir and chardonnay (as is most champagne). And like many champagnes, you can detect a little toastiness in the flavours, thanks to the length of time it spent on lees (yeast cells). Other than that, the flavours are well defined, the acidity is zesty and clean, and there's no lack of bubbles in the glass. Drink it as an aperitif or with seafood and chicken.

Cuvée Catharine Brut Sparkling Wine NV
VQA Niagara Peninsula 12% alc. $$$-$$$$

Featuring pinot noir and chardonnay, and made in the same method as champagne, this is a consistently reliable and high quality sparkling wine from Henry of Pelham. The flavours are solid and attractive, the acid bright, and the bubbles rise in steady beads from the bottom of the glass. It's a fizz to drink on its own or with food such as canapes, seafood, and poultry.

Cuvée Catharine Rosé Brut Sparkling Wine NV
VQA Niagara Peninsula 12% alc. $$$-$$$$

This is a lovely rosé sparkling wine that you can enjoy on its own or serve with roast turkey (or other poultry) when you want to dress up the table a little. But it's not just pretty—it's a pretty fabulous fizz. It's attractive mid-range pink in colour, and delivers equally attractive flavours that deliver very good complexity. The acidity is lively and crisp, as you want from sparkling wine, and the bubbles are fine, beaded, and plentiful.

Jackson-Triggs Grand Reserve 'Entourage' Sparkling Sauvignon Blanc 2015
VQA Niagara Peninsula 12% alc. $$$

This is a refreshing sparkling wine that benefits from the good natural acidity of sauvignon blanc. You'll find there's plenty of flavour and complexity in the fruit and that it's well balanced by the zesty acidity. There are plenty of persistent bubbles in the glass. This is dry but not so steely-dry that you can't enjoy it on its own. You can also pair it easily with seafood and white meats, or with appetizers of many kinds.

Tawse Winery 'Spark' Limestone Ridge Riesling Brut Sparkling Wine 2015
VQA Twenty Mile Bench, Ontario 12% alc $$$

Made from organically grown riesling grapes sourced from a single vineyard, this is a Traditional Method sparkling wine, with the second fermentation taking place in the bottle. As you'd expect from riesling, the wine has bright, zesty acidity, and here it's paired with defined and elegant flavours. It's a well-balanced fizz that you can drink on its own, as an aperitif, or with food.

Cono Sur Rosé Sparkling Wine NV
DO Valle del Bio Bio 12.5% alc. $$

This is made from pinot noir grapes grown in one of Chile's most southerly wine regions. The Bio Bio Valley is characterized by sunny days and cool temperatures, ideal conditions to produce grapes with the acidity needed for sparkling wine. This rosé fizz has lovely fresh flavours, zesty acidity, and all the bubbles you want. It's a wine you can drink on its own or take to the table to pair with chicken, turkey, or pork. It really perks up a Thanksgiving table.

FRANCE—CHAMPAGNE

Taittinger Réserve Brut Champagne NV
AOC Champagne 12.5% alc. $$$$$

At 40%, there's a higher proportion of chardonnay in this blended champagne than most—although champagnes labelled 'blanc de blancs' are generally 100% champagne. The blend here delivers a lot of elegance in the flavours, and it's well balanced by the crisp, clean acidity. There's plenty of bubble action, making this an excellent aperitif. If you want to pair it with food, think of seafood, white fish, pork, and poultry.

G.H. Mumm 'Cordon Rouge' Brut Champagne NV
AOC Champagne 12% alc. $$$$$

The 'cordon rouge', the red diagonal sash across the label, makes this champagne stand out on the shelf. It stands out for its quality/price ratio, too. It has a bright, substantial feel to it, and it's very drinkable. The flavours are multifaceted, the acidity is crisp and clean, and the bubbles perform extraordinarily well. It's not one of those steely champagnes you can't enjoy on its own, and you can drink it with many seafood, fish, and poultry dishes, too.

Laurent-Perrier Rosé Brut Champagne NV
AOC Champagne 12% alc. $$$$$

This is an iconic rosé champagne, far better-known than any of the many rosés made by champagne houses. It delivers everything you want and expect: concentrated flavours that are focused and defined, crisp and clean acidity, balance, and plenty of fine bubbles that rise in beads from the bottom of your glass. It has earned its reputation. This is a champagne you can sip on its own (hint: drink it from a regular wine glass, rather than a flute) or take it to the table and drink it with poultry and pork dishes.

Moët & Chandon Rosé Impérial Brut Champagne NV
AOC Champagne 12% alc. $$$$$

Moët & Chandon is one of the great champagne houses, producing a portfolio of vintage and non-vintage champagnes. Of course, you expect particular quality from the vintage-dated wines, but this is very high quality, none the less. It's dry, but not so dry that you can't enjoy it on its own, and it shows a great range of flavours. The acidity is vibrant and the bubbles are fine and beaded. It's an excellent choice for white meats and fish.

Perrier-Jouët 'Grand Brut' Brut Champagne NV
AOC Champagne 12% alc. $$$$$

This is a really lovely champagne that sings on its own or in the company of food. The flavours are rich, tiered, and well focused, and the texture is crisp and elegant. Here you find a winning tension between the brisk acidity and the roundness of the fruit, with hints of lees (dead yeast cells) flickering between. This is a fine aperitif, and it goes very well with many seafood, fish, poultry, and pork dishes.

Piper-Heidsieck Brut Champagne NV
AOC Champagne 12% alc. $$$$$

This is a very versatile champagne. You can pop the cork (not literally—always ease the cork so that it opens with a gentle hiss, not a pop, because the pop wastes bubbles) to celebrate birthdays, the launch of a battleship, and the like, or serve it with chicken, turkey, or pork. Dry and medium bodied with solid, complex flavours, and a refreshing texture, it delivers fine streams of bubbles that make for a clean, crisp mousse.

Pol Roger 'Extra Cuvée de Réserve' Brut Champagne NV
AOC Champagne 12.5% alc. $$$$$

This is very good champagne at a very good price. It has everything you look for in the animal: solid fruit flavours, complexity, a crisp and zesty texture, lots of fine bubbles steaming up from the bottom of the glass, and an edgy but quite soft mousse in the mouth. It's ideal as an aperitif, but you can take it to the table and drink it with many dishes from Asian cuisines, or with white meats and fish.

Taittinger 'Brut Réserve' Champagne NV
AOC Champagne 12.5% alc. $$$$$

Taittinger is a well-known champagne house for good reason. This example, made from pinot noir and chardonnay, is quite elegant in style, with well-defined and focused fruit flavours and a bright, zesty texture from the supporting acidity. Fine bubbles rise in beads, and the mousse is firm but yielding. This is an excellent champagne for food, and it goes well with many fish, seafood, and poultry dishes.

Veuve Clicquot Brut Champagne NV
AOC Champagne $$$$$

The distinctive yellow label makes Veuve Clicquot leap off the shelf visually—and leap off the shelf, literally, into the shopping carts of thousands of people daily. This is an excellent choice for many occasions because it delivers very good quality across the board. The flavours are focused and defined, the acidity is bright and correct, and the bubbles are many and fine. It's a great choice for an aperitif or for drinking with shellfish and other seafood.

Victoire 'Prestige' Brut Champagne NV
AOC Champagne 12% alc. $$$$$

Made by a cooperative winery in Champagne, this sells at an excellent price for the quality it delivers. The texture is crisp and bright, with good complexity and some yeasty notes, and the flavours are well layered and persistent right through the palate. It throws plenty of fine bubbles, forms a firm but gentle mousse, and is great sipped on its own or as an aperitif, or drunk with white meats and fish.

FRANCE—SPARKLING WINES
Château de Montgueret Brut Crémant de Loire
AOC Crémant de Loire 11.5% alc. $$-$$$

This sparkling wine from the Loire Valley, in northern France, is made by the method used to make champagne. It's a lovely blend of chenin blanc, chardonnay, and cabernet franc. It's slightly off-dry with attractive and complex flavours. With loads of fine bubbles, it's a perfect aperitif that will perk up your appetite. You can also drink it with spicy dishes in many Asian cuisines, such as garlic and ginger shrimp.

Pierre Sparr Brut Réserve Crémant d'Alsace
AOC Crémant d'Alsace 12.5% alc.   **$$-$$$**

This lovely sparkling wine, made in Alsace by the method used in Champagne, is made from the pinot blanc grape variety. It's dry, with just the right degree of fruitiness that enables you to drink it on its own, but has the acidity that makes it so versatile with food. The bubbles are fine and plentiful. Enjoy it as an aperitif or with well-seasoned or slightly spicy dishes that feature seafood, chicken, vegetables, and pork.

HUNGARY

Hungaria Grande Cuvée Brut NV
Hungary 12% alc.   **$$**

This represents very good value for a dry sparkling wine that's so versatile. The bright fruit flavours are quite complex and they're complemented by clean, refreshing acidity. There's plenty of bubble action in the glass. This is an easy choice if you're looking for a sparkling wine for mimosas or other mixed drinks, to sip on its own or as an aperitif, or to drink with chicken, white fish, or other lighter dishes.

ITALY

Astoria Extra Dry Prosecco
DOC Prosecco 11% alc.   **$$**

Prosecco has become immensely popular in the last few years as an affordable, easy-drinking sparkling wine. It has helped undermine the notion that sparkling wine is only for special occasions. This is a very good, dry prosecco, and a change from the fruitier style that is dominant. Look for attractive fruit flavours harnessed to bright acidity, and for plenty of bubbles in the glass. Sip it alone or drink it with poultry, pork, and fish dishes.

Bottega 'Il Vini dei Poeti' Brut
DOC Venezia 11.5% alc. $$

Bottega makes a number of popular sparkling wines, including the Vini dei Poeti series. This is a straightforward white sparkling wine that comes with pleasurable flavours, well-calibrated acidity, and plenty of bubble action in the glass. It's an easy choice for drinking on its own, as a base for cocktails, and for many lighter dishes that feature poultry, pork, white fish, and seafood.

Bottega 'Il vini dei poeti' Prosecco NV
DOC Prosecco 11% alc. $$

This is a mid-range prosecco that delivers everything you want from the style. It's essentially dry, with plenty of fruity flavours backed by crisp acidity. The bubbles are there in profusion and you can drink it easily on its own or with food. If you're thinking of food, fairly simple dishes such as roasted chicken and grilled white fish would be good candidates for this wine.

Bottega 'Il Vini dei Poeti' Rosé Brut Sparkling Wine
DOC Venezia 11.5% alc. $$

This is an attractive, fruit-driven, dry rosé sparkling wine that's well-price for the quality. Look for bright fruit flavours that pair well with the crisp acidity. There's plenty of bubble action in the glass. You'll find this is an easy wine to drink, either on its own or with food. It goes well with roast chicken and turkey, as well as with salads and fish burgers.

Chiarli Lambrusco NV
DOC Lambrusco Grasparossa di Castelvetro, Italy
8% alc. $$

Lambrusco is a lightly sparkling red wine mostly made in the area around Modena, which is also well known for balsamic vinegar. Although many lambruscos are now being made in a dry style most, like this one, have some sweetness. It's fruity, not too complicated, and has refreshing acidity, all of which make it an excellent wine for sipping on its own. But you can also pair it with spicy vegetarian, chicken, and pork dishes.

Mionetto Brut Prosecco NV
DOC Treviso 11% alc.   **$$**

This is a very attractive prosecco that delivers just what you want from a well-priced sparkling wine: it's easy-drinking and versatile. The flavours here are fresh and bright, rather like the well-balanced acidity, and there are plenty of bubbles in the glass. If you're looking for a sparkler for a large group, you won't go wrong with this. Sip it on its own or drink it with appetizers or with chicken, pork, and fish dishes.

Ruffino Prosecco NV
DOC Prosecco 11% alc.   **$$**

This is a fruity style of prosecco that might have some sweetness if it weren't taken care of by the acidity. Look for plenty of flavour here, a good dose of clean acidity, and a very good level of bubble activity in the glass. It's a versatile style that you can drink on its own, drink with chicken and pork and even with some spicy dishes made with them, and also use for making mimosas.

Villa Sandi 'Il Fresco' Prosecco NV
DOC Prosecco Treviso 11% alc.   **$$**

There are quite rich fruity flavours in this prosecco, a quality that often differentiates prosecco from its main rival, Cava, whose flavours tend to be a little more austere. Here they are supported by a seam of crisp, refreshing acidity, while the bubbles are plentiful and persistent. You can, of course, drink this on its own (the way I imagine most prosecco is consumed) but you could pair it with slightly spicy seafoods and chicken.

LUXEMBOURG

Bernard-Massard 'Cuvée de l'Écusson' Brut Sparkling Wine
Luxembourg 12.5% alc. $$

Not a well-known wine producing country, Luxembourg is none the less a significant producer of sparkling wine. This one delivers good quality across the board, with pleasant and reasonably layered flavours, very good acid-fruit balance, and plenty of small bubbles. Like most fizz, it can be drunk on its own or with food. As far as food is concerned, think of white meats and white fish, and it will also stand up to lightly spicy Thai and other Asian dishes.

NEW ZEALAND

Oyster Bay Sparkling Cuvée Brut
New Zealand 12% alc. $$

This is a really lovely dry sparkling wine that delivers well-defined fruit flavours and well-calibrated acidity. It's not the steely acidity you find in some sparkling wines, and it manages to combine edginess and drinkability. There's plenty of bubble action here, and you can enjoy this on its own, as an aperitif, or with seafood and white fish.

Oyster Bay Sparkling Cuvée Rosé
New Zealand 12.5% alc. $$

Poured into a glass, this is a very attractive salmon pink with plenty of beaded bubbles. But it's not just pretty to look at. It delivers lovely fruit flavours that are quite concentrated and decently complex and supported by crisp and clean acidity. It's fruity enough that you can enjoy it on its own, but dry enough to go very well with many dishes such as roast chicken or turkey, grilled salmon, and many salads.

Freixenet 'Carta Nevada' Premium Cava
DO Cava 11.5% alc. $$

Made in the method used for champagne (meaning it went through a fermentation in the very bottle you buy), this is a well-priced, good quality sparkling wine for many occasions. It's dry, has solid and concentrated flavours balanced with crisp acidity, and delivers plenty of bubbles. Drink it on its own, as an aperitif, with varied appetizers, and with poultry and seafood.

Freixenet 'Cordon Negro' Brut Cava
DO Cava 11.5% alc. $$

A slightly higher tier than Carta Nevada (above), this shows good complexity in the flavours and lively acidity. With the vigorous bubble activity, it makes for a refreshing sparkling wine you can enjoy on its own or with food. If you're thinking of the latter, think of all manner of seafood and white fish and creamy dishes featuring chicken or pork.

Segura Viudas Reserva Brut Cava
DO Cava 12% alc. $$

This is an excellent example of affordable cava. It's really dry and shows great fruit character, with flavours that are focused and well defined. The acidity is zesty and fresh, and there is very good bubble activity in the glass. Overall, it's balanced, attractive, and very drinkable. It's not so dry that you can't drink it on its own, but you can easily take it to the table when you're eating seafood, fish of all kinds, and poultry dishes,

He who knows how to taste does not drink wine but savours secrets.

- SALVADOR DALI

SWEET WINES

Cave Spring Riesling Icewine 2016
VQA Niagara Peninsula 11.5% alc. $$$$

[375mL] This is an icewine that delivers one of the best in the style, as you would expect from a producer that's well-known for its fine rieslings. There's plenty of flavour in the rich fruit, some light viscosity in the texture, and the trademark acidity of riesling. They are all well integrated here in a delicious wine you can sip on its own or pair with not-too-sweet desserts and blue cheese.

Cave Spring 'Indian Summer' Riesling
Select Late Harvest 2016
VQA Niagara Peninsula 12% alc. $$$

[375mL] This is not icewine, although the grapes were partly frozen when they were picked. They were left on the vine past the usual date when grapes were picked so they would lose water and shrivel. They were picked after the first frost. The result is rich, sweet flavours, but not as sweet as icewine, with vibrant acidity to cut through the sweetness. Sip it on its own or with fruit-based desserts.

Château des Charmes Vidal Icewine 2016
VQA Niagara-on-the-Lake 9.5% alc. $$$

[200mL] The vidal grape variety is often used to make icewine, and this example delivers all you expect from the style. Look for richness and sweetness in the flavours, but also fruitiness beyond the sweetness. The acidity is bright and clean, and it cuts through the richness effectively. Overall it's very well balanced and you can sip it alone or with rich foods such as foie gras or blue cheese.

Henry of Pelham Riesling Icewine 2015
VQA Niagara Peninsula 9.5% alc. $$$$$

[375mL] This has all the richness that almost totally frozen grapes can produce from the small volume of liquid sugar-filled juice that's left unfrozen. The threat of teeth-hurting and cloying sweetness is averted by the vibrant acidity. Chill it down in the fridge for 15-20 minutes (not too cold—it's called icewine but you don't want to drink it almost frozen!) and pair with briny blue cheese.

Inniskillin Vidal Icewine 2016
VQA Niagara Peninsula 10% alc. $$$$$

[375mL] Inniskillin, founded by Karl Kaiser and Donald Ziraldo in the 1970s, was the first Ontario winery to get a licence since the 1920s. It quickly became the standard-bearer of Canadian icewine, and the brand is widely recognized around the world. This vidal example delivers the sweet and pungent flavours you expect, along with well-pitched acidity needed to moderate the sweetness. Drink it with blue cheeses or foie gras.

Batosiolo 'Bosc dla Rei' Moscato d'Asti 2016
DOCG Moscato d'Asti 5.5% alc. $$

Made from the moscato grape variety, this is a luscious, moderately sweet white wine that goes well with desserts such as cheesecakes and fruit pies, as well as totally different food such as blue cheese and foie gras. You'll find it has a round texture with light viscosity, and that the bright acidity complements the fruit beautifully. It's a style that deserves wider appreciation.

UNITED STATES–CALIFORNIA

Obsession Symphony 2014
California 12% alc. $$

This is a moderately sweet white wine made from the symphony grape variety, which is an aromatic cross of the muscat of Alexandria and the grenache gris varieties. The flavours are quite intense and pungent, but a good dose of acidity takes care of much of the sweetness. It's a harmonious wine, as you would hope of one made from symphony. Chilled down, it goes very well with many spicy dishes from Asian culinary portfolios.

A bottle of wine contains more philosophy than all the books in the world.

- LOUIS PASTEUR

FRUIT WINES

CANADA

Cidrerie du Minot 'Crémant de Glace' Cidre Mousseux
Québec 7% alc. $$-$$$

[375mL] This is a sparkling ice cider that delivers the richness of ice cider but where the acidity and bubbles effectively reduce the sweetness. You get clear apple flavours that are quite complex, well-balanced and vibrant acidity, and a good level of effervescence. You can sip this on its own as a dessert wine or with not-too-sweet desserts. As you would expect, apple-based desserts go especially well with it.

Domaine Pinnacle Cidre de Glace/Ice Cider
Québec 12% alc. $$$

[375mL] Ice cider is made in roughly the same way as Icewine, by freezing the fruit (or juice) to separate the water (which freezes first). The unfrozen juice, which is very sweet, is then fermented to make this rich, sweet, somewhat viscous wine that has distinct apple flavours. Just as important, it has the keen acidity to keep the sweetness in check. Sip it on its own or drink it with not-too-sweet fruit (especially apple) desserts.

Southbrook Framboise

Ontario 14% alc. $$

[375mL] Made from the royalty variety of raspberries and fortified with a little eau-de-vie, this has become an icon. It's full of rich, intense, sweet raspberry flavours and has a slightly viscous texture. But the bright acidity cuts through the texture and the sweetness, making this amazingly drinkable. Try it with chocolate desserts, pour it over ice cream, or just sip it on its own.

SANTA RITA, MAIPO, CHILE

Where there is no wine,
there is no love.

- EURIPIDES

FORTIFIED WINES

PORT
Ferreira 'Dona Antonia' Reserva Tawny Porto
DOC Porto 20% alc. $$-$$$

Named for the head of the Ferreira port-producing family in the early 1800s, this is a luscious port that's delicious sipped on its own or with blue cheese and roasted nuts. It delivers sweet, rich, multilayered flavours and a texture that's slightly viscous and seems to swell in your mouth. But the acidity kicks in and kills much of the sweetness, leaving you with a long, complex, fruity finish.

Fonseca White Port
DOC Porto 20% alc. $$

Most port is red, but a small amount of white is made from white grape varieties growing in the Douro Valley. This one is very fruity, with a good range of flavours, and it's sweet in the port tradition. Chilled down, it's an excellent aperitif and you can also mix it with tonic water for a refreshing long drink.

Graham's 20-Year Tawny Port
DOC Porto 20% alc. $$$$-$$$$$

[500mL] To be labelled '10-Year' or '20-Year', ports don't need to spend that long in oak barrels; they need to achieve the quality and style a port typically would if it did. But these ports do have long aging ability, and this one shows it in its structure and the complexity and depth of its flavours. It's elegant, smooth and best appreciated on its own, at least for the first few sips. Then bring on the Stilton cheese.

Graham's Late Bottled Vintage Port 2012
DOC Porto, 20% alc.   **$$-$$$**

This is a very good example of LBV (Late Bottled Vintage) port, which is a high-quality port from a single year that is bottled after aging four to six years in barrels. LBVs are generally very good value, and this is definitely one of them. The flavours are rich, with controlled sweetness, and immensely complex. The acidity is right-on, making it a pleasure to drink. Sip it on its own or drink it with blue cheeses and dried fruits.

Sandeman Late Bottled Vintage Port 2012
DOC Porto 20% alc.   **$$**

True to its name, this is a port from the 2012 vintage. It was aged in oak for at least four years before being (late) bottled. It's a classic LBV, with depth and intensity in both flavours and texture. Lightly viscous, it shows plenty of complexity as it moves through your palate, and it's well balanced and lightly tannic. Port is one of the few wines that can go with (dark, high-cocoa) chocolate, so indulge!

Taylor Fladgate 20-Year-Old Tawny Port
DOC Porto 20% alc.   **$$$$$**

This port has been aged in oak for 20 years before being bottled. Over that time it has developed layers and layers of flavours that emerge within the essentially sweet port profile. The acidity is excellently calibrated to the fruit and sweetness, lightening the wine and making a second glass an easy proposition. You can drink this on its own or with Stilton or a Stilton-like blue cheese.

Warre's Otima 10 Ten-Year-Old Port
DOC Porto, Portugal 20% alc. $$$

[500 mL bottle] If you think of port as an after-dinner drink with the colour and weight of the leather armchairs favoured by the crusty old guys who drink it, try Otima. It's made in a lighter style—as you might expect from the colour, which is lighter than most ports—but it still has a full range of lovely sweet flavours. You can chill it and serve it as an aperitif or drink it less chilled after dinner with blue cheeses or dessert.

SHERRY
SPAIN
Dry Sack Medium Sherry
DO Jerez 19.5% alc. $$

Made from palomino and pedro ximénez grapes, this is an off-dry sherry that's excellent for sipping on its own or for drinking with snacks such as roasted nuts and dried fruits. They're among the flavours you'll find in this delightful and easy-drinking sherry, which is well-balanced and easy on your pocket, too.

Harvey's Bristol Cream Sherry
DO Jerez 17.5% alc. $$

This is a sweeter style of sherry, but it's absolutely not over-the-top sweet. It has quite a luscious texture, with some viscosity, and a real array of flavours. It's really for drinking on its own, ideally after being chilled slightly. Or you can pour it over ice cubes and garnish it with a twist of orange. It makes an excellent aperitif that way.

Lustau 'Los Arcos' Amontillado Sherry
DO Jerez 18.5% alc. $$

[375mL] This is a dry style of sherry with a little fruitiness alongside the classic rancio (oxidized) character. The flavour profile is dominated by dried fruits and its supported by a broad seam of diffuse, clean, acidity. Chill this down a little and sip it on its own or pair it with many Spanish tapas: fish, spicy sausages (such as chorizo), ham, grilled calamari, and the like.

Tio Pepe Extra Dry Fino Sherry
DO Jerez 15% alc. $$-$$$

Tio Pepe is an iconic fino sherry. Made in an astringently dry style ("extra dry" is an understatement), it has pungent, high-toned flavours backed by bright, taut acidity. Chill it down slightly. Although it's not to everyone's taste when drunk on its own, it's an excellent partner for many Spanish tapas—dishes such as olives, almonds, grilled calamari, Serrano ham, and chorizo.

ABOUT THE AUTHOR

Rod Phillips is a wine writer, author, and judge based in Ottawa, and Professor of History at Carleton University, where he teaches courses on the history of alcohol and food. He is wine writer and contributing editor of *NUVO Magazine* (Canada), writes for *Vines Magazine* (Canada) and occasionally contributes to *The World of Fine Wine* (UK) and GuildSomm.com (US). He wrote the *500 Best-Value Wines in the LCBO* annually from 2008 to 2017, and he is the author of a number of other books on wine, including *French Wine: A History* (2016), *The Wines of Canada* (2017), *9000 Years of Wine: A World History* (2017), and *Wine: A Social and Cultural History of the Drink that Changed Our Lives* (2018). He was the weekly wine columnist for the *Ottawa Citizen* from 2001 to 2016, and he regularly visits wine regions around the world.